FAMILY HEALING:

Healing Family Hurts

PAULIST PRESS
New York, N.Y./Ramsey, N.J.

Photo Credits
Miriam Berkley: 105
Craig Callan: 115
Janice Canova: 18
Mia et Klaus: 82
Rick Smolan: 32; 56

Designer: Gloria Ortíz

Nihil Obstat
Msgr. Carroll E. Satterfield
Censor Librorum

Imprimatur
Most Rev. William D. Borders, D.D.
Archbishop of Baltimore
October 31, 1979

Library of Congress
Catalog Card Number: 79-90991

IBSN: 0-8091-2266-9

Published by Paulist Press
Editorial Office: 1865 Broadway, New York, N.Y. 10023
Business Office: 545 Island Road, Ramsey, N.J. 07446

Printed and bound in the
United States of America

Contents

INTRODUCTION

The stories in *Healing Family Hurts* are real stories about real people. The problems which are described here may never be our problems. But we know from statistics and perhaps from our own experience that these problems exist and affect many individuals and families today.

When we read the gospels, we see that Jesus' ministry was primarily a healing ministry. He healed physical problems, but also brought wholeness to people who suffered because they were outcasts in society or broken in spirit. The causes of this rejection and brokenness in Jesus' time were perhaps different from our own. As followers of Jesus we are invited to be healers. We are called to approach the problems of our day in the same way that Jesus approached the problems of his.

In Jesus' time, the poor and afflicted were thought to deserve their suffering because of some sin on their part or that of their ancestors. Today we think of such an attitude as primitive, based on ignorance about physical and emotional problems. But we run the risk of adopting a similar attitude if we do not try to understand the causes and effects of contemporary problems. If, for example, we believe that alcoholics drink because they like to, or that the poor are poor because they are too lazy to be otherwise, then we really do not understand the nature of problems such as alcoholism and poverty. The first step in being a healer is to understand the nature of the problems we are dealing with. The essays in *Healing Family Hurts* have as their first function descriptions of contemporary problems that will enable us to learn the facts of the situation. In this way we can learn to understand and be sympathetic about these problems.

Another dimension of Jesus' ministry which is clear in the gospels is that he was a man who was deeply involved in his community and understood its needs. The healing that takes place between Jesus and an individual is on one level very personal. Yet on a broader level this healing always takes place in a communal context. Jesus calls the community around him to change its attitude toward those who are hurting. In the same way today there is a need for the involvement of the whole community in understanding and healing. Problems like divorce, addiction, physical abuse, and death affect individuals and their families. But these problems also affect the entire community. *Healing Family Hurts* examines ways that the local community can be a source of healing to those who are in need of it.

ASSESSING FAMILY PROBLEMS

Fran Ferder

Almost 2000 years ago, a family we have come to call holy began their life together. It started with a crisis—a pregnancy that had not been planned and a confused young groom considering a quiet divorce. Soon there was another problem—an unexpected business trip at the worst of all possible times. All the carefully made plans suddenly changed. There was an uncomfortable journey and a lonely birth. The difficulties must have seemed endless to this young couple: frightening threats on their child's life; moving without a moment's notice; and then, moving again just when things seemed to be settling down. Later, there was the adolescent crisis—the teenager who wandered off, at first frightening his parents with his unexplained absence, then bewildering them with his plans for the future. Eventually, death touched their lives. At some point the father died, leaving his widow—a parent alone—with all the heartache and emptiness that follows death. The child, the searching adolescent, had become an adult. He was different, not accepted. The neighbors didn't like his life-style. They disapproved of the company he kept. They grew to hate him. And, finally, they murdered him. The family unit was gone now. Only the widow was left. She grew old. Alone.

Mary, Joseph, and Jesus were a family much like any of our families today. They knew fear, loneliness, confusion, disagreement, and disappointment. Sometimes, in our religious fervor, we may tend to spiritualize away the full and painful impact of the problems they faced by believing that they had direct access to solutions through angels and dreams. The fact is that they *were* close to God, a God who spoke to them through the persons and events of their lives. But our families today have the same access to this same God. The God who led them out of crisis beckons us also. Their God—our God—is a God who reaches out to human pain and still speaks through the persons and events of human life.

This program will explore some of the ways that families can increase their ability to assess problems that confront them. It will not provide specific solutions for specific problems. Rather, it will aid families in becoming more aware of the importance of looking at family life reflectively, admitting what they see there. It will stress that our God is no foreigner to family crises, but one who reaches out to touch pain with healing. It will present a simple reflective method for:

a) developing an attitude of nondefensive openness to family problems;
b) accepting and admitting problems when they exist;
c) naming problems specifically and identifying their source;
d) evaluating the seriousness of the problem;
e) making a decision to explore solutions.

"HOW IS IT THAT YOU DO NOT KNOW HOW TO INTERPRET THESE TIMES?"

Why is it so important to assess our family life? Why should we evaluate the problems we face? There are several reasons. First, we need to know if the problem we are experiencing is caused by an event or circumstance beyond our immediate control or if we have contributed to its development. Does it result from persons, situations, or accidents that we cannot prevent or change? For example, the birth of a handicapped child causes a crisis that was not determined by human behavior. Once it has occurred we cannot change the basic facts of the situation. We can only muster our energies to cope with it.

In contrast, there are some types of problems that we have helped to cause, at least in part, by our own unhealthy response to life. It is often within our control to reduce or eliminate the problem by changing our behavior. If I have created an atmosphere of fear and tension in the family because I have an uncontrollable temper, I can reduce the tension by facing my temper and changing the way I respond to anger. In this situation, I devote my energy not to *coping* with an irreversible problem or forcing others to cope with unnecessary tension, but to *eliminating* the problem. It is important, then, to know whether we face an unchangeable situation—or a changeable one—if we are to use our energies effectively. It is also important to know which family member faces primary responsibility for changing a form of behavior in those situations requiring a change. Assessment can help us determine this.

A second reason for assessment is to help us ascertain whether or not we are handling family problems in a growthful way. Are we facing and dealing with them, or are we failing to handle the situation adequately? Facing and dealing with tensions and problems means that we reflect on the situation, its cause, and the people it affects. Another way of saying that we are "facing" a problem is by saying that we "look it in the face." We explore it. We allow ourselves to experience feelings about it. We talk about it with each other or with someone we can trust. The next section will focus more on the steps involved in doing this.

Handling a problem in a way that is not growthful means that we behave toward it in a manner that does not move us toward a successful resolution. Some examples of responses that are not growthful are:

a) ignoring the problem completely and/or refusing to discuss it;
b) blaming others for the problem;
c) withdrawing from other family members and friends;
d) having outbursts of uncontrollable anger;
e) covering up the effects of the problem and/or making excuses for it;
f) worrying privately about it;
g) becoming irritable and anxious;
h) developing physical symptoms, such as headaches and stomach problems, in response to the situation.

There are two common extremes that people often fall into when confronted with problems that are longstanding. One extreme is to think about the problem constantly, bringing it up in every conversation, discussing it with anyone who will listen. The second is to deny the problem altogether, refusing to talk about it or to think about it. Both extremes are unhealthy. Both drive people away.

Dealing with a problem growthfully, then, means that we give enough attention to it to allow us to work toward its resolution while avoiding these two extremes.

A third—and perhaps more important—reason for assessing family problems is to take an honest look at the role we are allowing God to play in the situation, not just in the problem, but in the whole of our family life. When we suddenly face a crisis and find ourselves begging God to help us resolve it, we ought to ask, *How long has it been since I (or we) talked personally to God?* Do we go to God just when we have problems, much as we would go to the medicine cabinet for a Band-Aid when we get cut, or is God a regular part of the family consciousness? Developing a habit of assessing the health of our family life gives us an automatic opportunity to also evaluate our relationship to God.

"SHE KEPT ALL THESE THINGS, PONDERING THEM IN HER HEART"

The first step in assessing family problems involves a *willingness* to take an honest look at my family life—not the neighbors' or the relatives'—but mine, *ours.* It might be described as developing an attitude of nondefensive openness. It is done through quiet reflection on the everydayness of our life together. I simply allow myself to think about what is happening in my family. As I think, I let my mind float clearly over the many aspects of our life, and I make a conscious decision to see it as it really is. I ask myself revealing questions:

a) What is the predominant mood of our family? (For example, are we basically happy or sad? Are we relaxed or tense with each other?)
b) How do I feel and act toward each member of my family? Why? (Think about each member individually.)

c) How do other family members seem to feel and act toward me? Why? (Again, think about each member individually.)

d) What causes tension in our family? How do we handle the tension?

e) What do I contribute to the tension?

It is very important to allow ourselves to reflect in this manner in order to gain an accurate picture of our family life. The questions ought to be reflected on privately, but could then be discussed during a family meeting or informal sharing time.

This kind of reflection ought to be done on a fairly regular basis, just as regularly as one would reflect on the family's financial status or physical health. Too often, families who are experiencing minor tensions fail to take time to look at their lives reflectively. They are unaware that small problems are developing. As a result, small tensions mount over the months and years, developing into major and sometimes irresolvable conflicts. Few adults would consistently ignore a steadily dwindling bank account without making some adjustments in the family's spending patterns or seeking some form of financial help. Few adults would put off medical care for a child with a high fever. Yet many families ignore or put off dealing with problems that can cripple the emotional and spiritual health in the home.

Periodic reflection, with an openness to really see what is happening in the family, will enable us to identify small problems while they are still small. It will also help us choose our responses to problems rather than react to them impulsively at the moment they loom before us. For example, let us say that twelve-year-old Billy is beginning to keep company with some high school boys of questionable reputation. It would be much better for me to reflect on this situation during a moment of quiet, asking myself what I might do to help Billy, why he might be doing this, etc., rather than yell at him the next time he is on his way out the door to meet with his new friends. Often, we "blow up" or respond nongrowthfully in those situations we have not taken time to reflect on earlier.

"THE TRUTH WILL SET YOU FREE"

The second step in assessing family problems involves *accepting* what I see. It is vital that I *own* the problem or problems I have identified through the process of reflection. I do this by admitting, first to myself, perhaps even out loud, "*We* do *have a problem—we* are *hurting—there is a part of our family life that needs healing.*" Once I can do this, I am able to experience an amazing new freedom inside. I am no longer spending a great deal of energy hiding problems and tensions from myself. This means that I have more energy available to work on the problem.

"SEEK AND YOU SHALL FIND"

A third step in assessing family problems involves identifying—specifically—their source. It means giving a name to the problem. Sometimes this is easy because the problem is obvious, and the tensions surrounding it are quickly visible. Such is the case involving a sudden crisis or a problem that is highly developed, e.g., a child is killed in a car accident or a young father is dying of cancer. In each of these, or similar cases, we can readily name the crisis and see how it affects each member of the family. A parent is tearful and preoccupied at work for several weeks following the death of the child. A high school student's grades drop because of the dying father. A younger child acting up in school could be directly related to either of these crisis situations.

Other times, naming a specific problem is more difficult because the problem is more subtle. We cannot seem to see a cause for the conflicts we are experiencing. This is characteristic of problems that develop over time. We may only know that we feel distant from each other or that we've grown apart. We are not sure why. There may be communication problems associated with this kind of situation. We can't talk to each other without fighting. We avoid each other. We don't feel close. There hasn't been a crisis or a single major problem. Still, we are unhappy with how our family life is going.

In situations such as these it might be helpful to express our feelings to other members of the family, to share our concerns. This is done by *reflecting ahead of time* on our feelings and then naming them out loud: "I've been feeling distant from you lately. It seems that we just aren't spending much time together anymore."

If we can engage other family members in conversation and encourage them to share their feelings in this manner (while we listen without interrupting or contradicting), it is possible, over a period of time, to discover together what is wrong. It is possible to name the problem. If, on the other hand, other family members (or a member) are not able or willing to explore the situation with us, it can be helpful to talk with a person outside the family about our feelings. This person might be a trusted friend or counselor.

"MY SOUL IS TROUBLED UNTO DEATH"

The fourth step in assessing family problems involves *evaluating the seriousness* of the pain. For example, what kind of impact does the problem have on each member of the family, children as well as adults? Who is most affected by the problem and how seriously? Is anyone in the family unable to continue their routine responsibilities because of the problem? Can we handle it alone, or do we need some additional support?

All normal and well-adjusted families experience tension, crises, and problems from time to time. However, these daily tensions or occasional crisis situations should generally not incapacitate any member of the family for a long period of time. They should not provide a permanent interference with functioning in school, at home, on the job, or in religious and social life. Ten-year-old Susie might have a stomach ache and stay home from school the day her older sister moves away to college. This is a normal adjustment reaction. It would not be regarded as serious. Other than providing the child with warmth and understanding, we should not make an issue of her reaction. However, if she develops nightmares, stops eating, and refuses to attend school for several weeks, this is much more critical. Her reaction is out of proportion to the event. It would be well for Susie's parents to talk to an understanding friend, pastor, teacher, or counselor about her behavior.

Some questions to ask in the face of a crisis or problem situation in order to evaluate its seriousness are:

a) *Is the person or family reacting to the problem in a manner that seems inappropriate to its severity?*
For example, we would expect seventeen-year-old Bob to be very upset about his parents' sudden divorce. We would not, however, expect him to become violent and physically abusive toward his younger brother and sister as a result.

b) *Does the reaction seem to be lasting longer than it should?*
For example, it would be quite normal for Mr. Jones to grieve severely over the death of his wife of thirty years. It would not be normal to find him in the same stage of grief five years later.

c) *Is the person or family incapacitated by the problem?*
For example, if Mary drinks a bit too heavily on occasion but manages to carry on with her responsibilities, we would not consider her drinking an incapacitating problem at this stage (though it could become so). If, on the other hand, she is drunk much of the time by midafternoon, and if her husband and children are covering up for her, we would consider her (and possibly her family) incapacitated by the problem of alcoholism.

If we answer "yes" to any or all of these questions, we can assume that we are dealing with a problem or crisis that has some serious aspects. In such a case, it can be supportive to seek the understanding support or counsel of a pastor or professional counselor.

"GET UP, PICK UP YOUR SLEEPING MAT AND WALK"

The fifth and final step in assessing family problems involves exploring solutions. An important consideration here is the timing of the problem. If the problem is new and sudden, of crisis proportions, such as a teen-age pregnancy, immediate attention is automatically focused on the problem. Because of their urgency, crisis situations cause us to mobilize our resources, look for solutions, and act quickly.

However, when problems have been building for a long time and do not present themselves to us in one drastic moment, it is easier to postpone dealing with them. When the disease of alcoholism is developing; when conflicts with teen-agers are beginning; when a marriage relationship starts to feel strained, we so often want to believe that "things will get better." Sometimes we cling desperately to the hope that things will get better on their own because we don't know how to help them get better. We feel guilty, helpless, confused, ashamed.

Exploring solutions always means talking out loud about the problem within the family. Opening up the issue is a first step toward healing. When discussing the problem within the family is impossible, at least initially, talking about it with an outside person becomes necessary. Talk should center around things each family member can do, both alone and together, to help the situation.

Exploring solutions can also be done through reading materials or books that deal with the particular problem your family is experiencing. For example, if the problem is alcoholism, the family may gain much insight by reading one or some of the many resource pamphlets on the disease available at most libraries or local counseling agencies.

In addition to reflecting, talking with others, and reading, solutions to family problems need to be explored through prayer. Families need to pray together for healing. They need to expose themselves to God's intervention in their lives. They need to read Scripture, allowing it to give them insights and move them toward action.

Once we have reflected on our family life, opened ourselves to its reality, named problems, examined their seriousness, and explored solutions, we must make a firm decision to follow what we have come to know about ourselves. Assessment only begins the journey of family growth. We must not simply identify problems, then sit back. We must walk forward, changing what needs changing, getting support and help where necessary. We must keep before us the belief that our God is a God who reaches out to human pain.

> . . . submit to the word which has been planted in you. . . . But you yourselves must do what the word tells you, and not just listen to it and deceive yourselves. To listen to the word and not obey is like looking at your own features in a mirror and then, after a quick look, going off and immediately forgetting what you looked like. But the person who looks steadily at the perfect law of freedom and makes that his habit, not listening and then forgetting, but actively putting it into practice, will be happy in all that he does (James 1:21–25).

FRAN FERDER, FSPA, Ph.D. Sister Fran is a clinical psychologist and is involved in family ministry consultation, communications, and human relations. She is author of *Called to Break Bread?*, a psychological study of women who feel called to the Catholic priesthood, and is co-director of the Quixote Center.

ALCOHOLISM: A CHRISTIAN PERSPECTIVE

Regina M. Ryan

Alcoholism is a disease that affects the lives of millions of Americans each year. In the *Third Special Report to the U.S. Congress on Alcohol and Health*, the Department of Health, Education, and Welfare estimated the number of alcoholics at 9 to 10 million people. Others who work with alcoholics and their families believe that the figure is much higher. They suggest a figure of 20 to 25 million alcoholics, affecting the lives of 100 million people, half the population of the United States.

The numbers alone suggest that the Christian community should be aware of the problems encountered by families living with alcoholism. In some way, the disease touches most of our lives—at home, at work, or among friends. As Christians called to follow Christ in his healing mission, we hope to become better informed about the disease of alcoholism and its effects on family life. We will pray, reflect, and do what we can to mend the broken hearts, to free the captives.

The following discussion is not intended to directly aid alcoholic families. It will focus on five main areas:

1) The Moral Question
2) Effects On Family Life
3) There Is Hope
4) Alcoholics Look At The Church
5) The Christian Response—What Can We Do?

THE MORAL QUESTION

We've come a long way in overcoming some of the ill-founded prejudices that were common during the life of Christ. We would laugh at the suggestion that a leper is an immoral person who has been physically punished by God.

And what of the disciples' question about the sins of the blind man? In this age of modern medicine would a Christian condemn a person because he is afflicted with a disease? Would we cast the afflicted out of our homes, sneer at them behind their backs, or speak ill of them in the presence of their families? Would we put a stigma on a disease that is so horrible, so shameful, that sick persons become afraid to seek treatment and die?

What about alcoholics? Alcoholics suffer from a disease. Their condition was formally recognized by the American Medical Association in 1956. Research has shown that alcoholism is a disease with recognizable symptoms and that it continues to get worse unless treated. Scientists now know that alcoholics are not immoral people who can but won't control their drinking. Nor are alcoholics suffering from underlying psychological or emotional disorders that cause their alcoholism.

Alcoholics who are not treated do die. Each year thousands become victims of cirrhosis, heart disease, cancer, accidents, violent crime, and suicide because of alcohol addiction. Why are the lives of so many men, women, and teenagers wasted? Recovered alcoholics, and those who work with alcoholics and their families, agree that the biggest single obstacle that keeps alcoholics and families from seeking the help they need is the stigma attached to the disease.

How do you get the disease? No one knows for sure, but this is what is known:

a) Most people who drink alcoholic beverages never develop alcoholism. A 1971 report to the U.S. Congress from the Department of Health, Education, and Welfare stated that one out of thirteen who drink alcoholic beverages will become alcoholics.
b) Alcoholism does not develop without drinking alcohol, but the beverage by itself is not enough to bring on the disease.
c) Alcoholism affects all types of people. The disease respects no ethnic, economic, social, religious, or geographic lines. Only 3 to 5 percent of American

alcoholics fit the skid row stereotype. The rest are housewives, laborers, students, executives, farmers, preachers, doctors, and lawyers. There is no such thing as a typical alcoholic.

Recent studies have focused on the family. There is a higher rate of alcoholism among relatives of alcoholics than in the general population. Some of these findings suggest that genetic factors are involved. There is also evidence that the risk of alcoholism is increased by family conditions that damage the bonds between parent and child. But at this time, there is no conclusive evidence to prove the causes of alcoholism.

In summary, medical research has shown that the alcoholic is suffering from a disease, not a moral problem. If a moral problem does exist, it must rest with the community that creates or tolerates an atmosphere that prevents alcoholics and their families from seeking treatment.

EFFECTS ON FAMILY LIFE

Alcoholism is a disease that affects the whole family. As the disease progresses, the alcoholic becomes more and more detached from anything and anyone who stands in the way of drinking. As a result, relationships with family members can become strained or neglected completely, and friends may back off. The alcoholic may lose a job, or a house, or a spouse. Through all this, the alcoholic may try to be perfectly charming, or stubbornly self-righteous. These are merely defenses built to protect the alcoholic from the real inner feelings: guilt, shame, fear, pain, hurt.

Each family member reacts to the disease. Someone, usually a spouse, assumes the role of the "Enabler." The Enablers take on all financial responsibilities, try to protect the alcoholic, and keep the family together. Very often they blame themselves for the spouses' drinking problem. One minute the Enabler may appear to be Superperson; the next, a self-pitying, powerless person with little or no self-confidence. The Enabler, too, is working to hide true inner feelings: anger, guilt, pain, fear, hurt.

The children take on different roles, each searching for

Involvement of Alcohol in Injuries and Unnatural Deaths

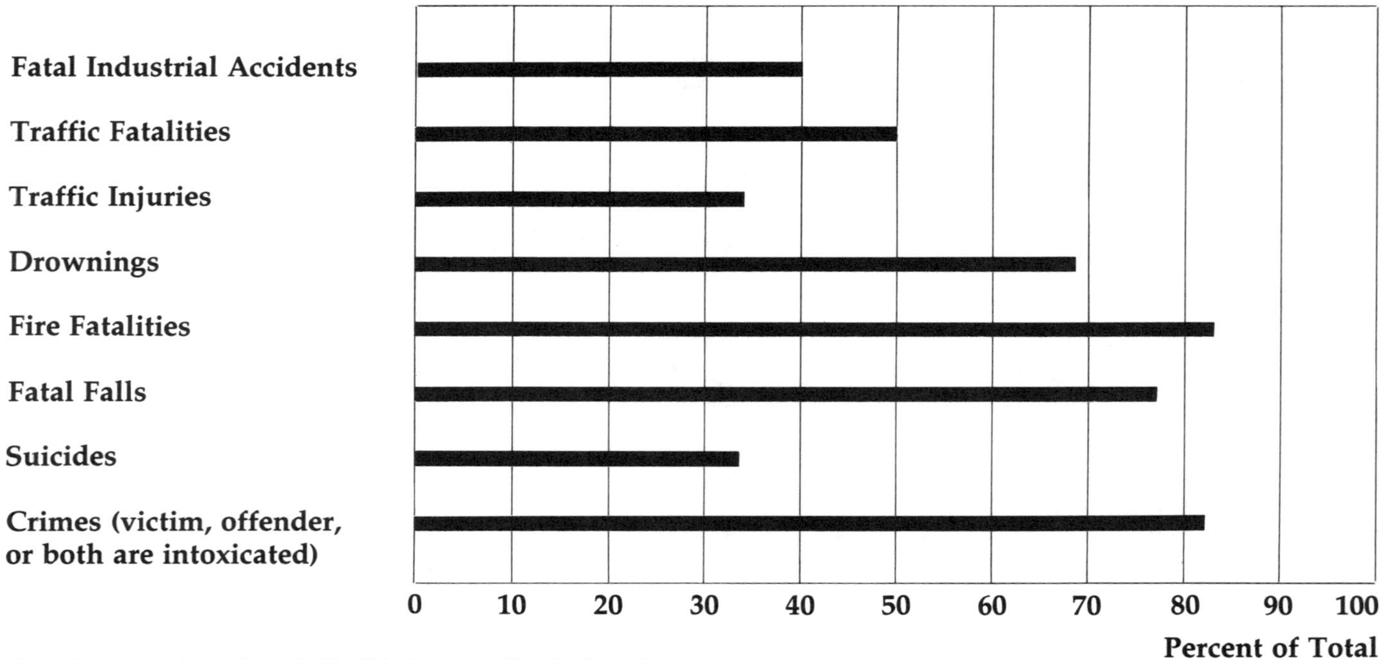

Source: *Summary of the 3rd Report To The U.S. Congress on Alcohol and Health from the Secretary of Health, Education, and Welfare*, National Institute on Alcohol and Alcohol Abuse (NIAAA) Information and Feature Service, (November 30, 1978)

a way to avoid pain. One may be very independent and responsible, another withdrawn. Others may experiment with juvenile delinquency, or become hyperactive and try to attract attention. These children are covering up a range of inner feelings: anger, loneliness, inadequacy, insecurity, hurt, and confusion.

Moral judgments cast upon the family by other relatives can complicate the situation for the whole family. Children trying to understand the illness of someone they love is hard enough. Unfortunately, many children become the dumping ground for adults in the family who burden them with hurtful remarks aimed indirectly at the alcoholic. Some may make the children feel as if they have to choose between "right" and parent. Here comes that old moral stigma again. It is not merely a factor outside the family. It also plays a part in the family confusion.

Let us take a brief look at an alcoholic family. It is a story of a difficult situation, but it is also a hopeful story because this family survived. Carol and Joe were in their early forties when everything seemed to be falling apart. They had been married twenty years and had three children: Jim, seventeen; Barbara, fifteen; and Kathy, twelve. Carol is an alcoholic.

Carol had her first drink when she was eighteen, a freshman in college. She drank socially during those years away at school, overdid it at times, but never felt that she had a problem. Right after graduation, she married Joe. They both got good jobs and seemed like the perfect couple, getting ahead in life. After their first child was born, Carol quit her job and stayed home to raise a family. While the children were very young, she drank regularly, but no one was alarmed. She managed to confine her drinking to the hours when Joe was at work, and the kids were either asleep or in school.

Gradually Carol's drinking increased until the children were returning from school and finding her passed out on the sofa. If Joe questioned her condition, she claimed to have a virus. The situation deteriorated rapidly. Jim came home after school and cooked dinner. Barbara found after-school activities that managed to keep her out of the house as much as possible. Kathy was always running in and out of the house, trying but never quite succeeding in her efforts to get Mom and Dad to laugh.

Joe was becoming a nervous wreck. He was Super Dad at home—managing the household chores, supervising homework assignments, persuading friends and relatives that nothing was wrong. But at work he was not able to concentrate. He spent most of his time worrying, wondering if Carol was drinking. It was his fault, of course. He had driven his wife to drink, and now he couldn't stop her. He was losing his confidence and it showed in his work.

And those kids! Why were the kids becoming such a problem, just when all he could handle was Carol? Jim, an excellent student, was not getting into any serious difficulty, but his grades began to drop, and he seemed to have lost his direction, his drive. It was several years later before Jim recovered his sense of direction.

Barbara was flirting with trouble. She was staying out later and later and neglecting her studies. If Carol or Joe reprimanded her, she always replied that they of all people were in no position to criticize her. There were a number of brushes with the local police who suspected Barbara was involved with drug sales at her high school.

Kathy knew Mom and Dad were unhappy. She wanted them all to be happy again. All anyone seemed to do anymore was worry about Mom and yell at Barbara. Kathy became the family clown. Her jokes rarely got a laugh at home, but she kept trying.

To make matters worse, Joe's parents kept complaining about Carol. Nothing could convince them that Carol was sick. Too bad she wasn't like Joe's sister-in-law, who drank like a lady and cared about her family. To this day, Joe doubts that they understand how much their put-downs of Carol hurt him and the children.

For some time now, an old friend of Carol's who was active in Alcoholics Anonymous had been trying to get her to come to a meeting. But Carol wasn't like "those people." Inside, however, she was afraid to admit she needed help. After a serious car accident, Carol finally decided to give AA a chance. She had a rough few months, but she's been sober for six years. She looks younger. She's healthy, and her confidence in herself shows.

Joe started attending Al-Anon meetings while Carol was still drinking. He became visibly stronger as he came to believe that Carol was sick and that her drinking had nothing to do with him. He realized that all his worrying didn't affect Carol's drinking. His work showed an improvement, and he was much more at ease with the children.

The children came through their difficulties that were related to alcoholism as they learned more about the disease and how it was affecting their lives.

Someone just meeting this family would not be able to see that they are in any way different from a nonalcoholic family. In many ways they seem stronger. Each family member has developed his/her own strengths. They are not without their problems. They are not without their scars. But they are learning to find their own paths, one day at a time.

THERE IS HOPE

Alcoholics Anonymous saved Carol's life and has saved the lives of millions of other alcoholics. She admitted that she was powerless over alcohol, put her faith in a power greater than herself, and became part of the oldest and largest program for controlling alcoholism. AA is a voluntary fellowship of over a million alcoholics whose sole aim is to get themselves and others sober, and to stay sober. Membership is open to anyone who has a problem with alcohol.

AA uses a spiritual approach to overcome the addiction to alcohol and depends on the commitment of its members to help each other. AA members meet regularly in small groups across the country. Open meetings may be attended by the public. Closed meetings are limited to AA members.

Al-Anon Family Groups and Alateen were set up to help relatives and friends of alcoholics deal with the problems in their own lives that may arise because of alcoholism. Membership is open to relatives and friends of alcoholics, whether or not the alcoholic is a member of AA. All Al-Anon and Alateen meetings are limited to members.

Lite

A relatively new concept in the treatment of alcoholism is called "intervention." It was developed at the Johnson Institute in Minneapolis. During an intervention, an alcoholic is confronted with concrete evidence of his/her drinking problem by people who are important in his/her life, such as family members, friends, and employer. The aim of the intervention is to halt the progression of the disease by getting the alcoholic to recognize the drinking problem and to agree to seek treatment. If the intervention is successful, the alcoholic is referred to local treatment centers, counseling, and AA. Family counseling programs are also available.

There is hope for alcoholics. Millions of alcoholics have recognized their disease, their limitations, and put their faith in a higher power. And once they have recovered, they in turn are strengthening their brothers and sisters.

ALCOHOLICS LOOK AT THE CHURCH

Has the Christian community done enough to help our brothers and sisters who are alcoholics? Four AA members, all practicing Catholics, were asked how the Church helped them or hurt them in overcoming alcoholism, and how the Church could have been more helpful. Here are their replies.

Jane: I never would have sought help at my parish. I have no doubt that I would have been called a bad person. My recommendation to parish staff and parishioners would be to 1) learn more about alcoholism, and 2) to refer calls for help to AA or someone they know in AA unless they are a member themselves.

Bob: My experience is that the Catholic Church would rather ignore alcoholism. I think that religious leaders should first look at their own priests and religious. Not enough is being done to help alcoholic priests and religious.

Jack: The Catholic Church doesn't want to have anything to do with AA. Very rarely are Catholic facilities offered for AA and Al-Anon meetings. There are always a lot of Catholics at those meetings, but with few exceptions, they are held in Protestant churches. Is the Church afraid of us? I think Catholics could be more helpful if they extended a welcome mat to AA. Pastors or parish councils could ask AA members to set up a core group in the parish that would respond to calls for help.

Linda: I had a good experience. I called the rectory while I was drinking to get a little sympathy. I talked to an AA priest and he brought me to my first meeting.

SUGGESTIONS FOR FURTHER ACTION

1. **Educate.** Learn more about alcoholism and encourage others to do the same. Your public library is a good resource. Attend an open AA meeting in your area. Call the Alcoholics Anonymous number in your phone book for information.
2. **Extend a Welcome.** Do AA groups use your parish facilities? Contact AA and extend a welcome.
3. **Refer to Competent Help.** What happens if someone in your parish calls for help with a drinking problem? Find out. Explore ideas on how AA can help.
4. **Monitor Local Health Facilities.** Does your community have a facility for treating alcoholics who need emergency care? Is it adequate? Are hospitals with state and federal funding breaking the law by denying alcoholics emergency room treatment?
5. **Develop and Encourage Programs to Aid Recovered Alcoholics.** A group in New York City called the Employment Program for Recovered Alcoholics (EPRA) is a pioneer group doing comprehensive career counseling and job placement for men and women who have recovered from the disease of alcoholism. Would such a service help recovered alcoholics in your area? If you are in New York could you refer people to EPRA for help? Could you contact EPRA with job openings? Explore other ways that we can help restore the recovered alcoholic to full participation in the life of our communities.
6. **Pray for Healing.** Pray that alcoholics and their families will be healed. Pray for the Christian community—for what we have done, and for what we have failed to do.

CHRISTIANS IN A LAND OF MILK AND HONEY AND DRUGS

Regina M. Ryan

Drugs. They are as American as apple pie. Since the 1960s we have heard more and more about drug use, particularly among adolescents and young adults. We have read pamphlets, listened to the latest rumors, watched the documentaries. At times it may seem like another world—"out there." For some of us the drug world is closer. We may have already been called to a hospital or police station to support a family member or a friend. Or we may be waiting in fear for that phone call.

We in the Christian community have not been untouched by drug abuse in our families, our schools, our communities. We have not always been as informed as we should be, and our response to drug abuse has not always been without panic and anger. If we are to respond as Christians faced with a widespread problem, we must proceed calmly and compassionately.

The drug problem is complex. There are different kinds of drugs being used. There are different kinds of drug users. There are a host of theories offered by "experts" on what constitutes problem use, and what are appropriate responses to drug use. It is very easy to get confused.

This article will deal in a very general way with a few key issues relating to mood-changing drugs. We are not concerned here with drugs that are prescribed by a doctor, taken by the patient in the specified amount and within a specified time to treat a particular condition. We will not, however, limit discussion to illegal drugs. Mood-changers can be found as over-the-counter preparations and prescription drugs as well.

People use drugs differently, so all drug users will not be considered as one big problem group. Distinctions are made among experimental, recreational, regular, and dependent users.

Experimental users are people who try a drug once or twice out of curiosity.

Recreational users are people who use drugs to be social at parties, to get high with friends.

Regular users are people who are almost always under the influence of a drug while trying to maintain normal activities (school, work, etc.).

Dependent users are people whose world centers on drug taking. They experience physical or mental discomfort if withdrawn from drugs.

The most widely abused drugs are caffeine, tobacco, and alcohol, but they will not be discussed in any detail here. Alcohol has been treated separately, and accurate information on the effects of nicotine addiction has been well publicized since the Surgeon General's Report on Smoking and Health was published in 1964. These familiar drugs will be used to some extent, however, to put the whole drug picture into perspective.

This article is not intended to give a parent or concerned person all he or she needs to know about drugs. It is hoped that it will open positive discussions, prompt further reading, and lead to compassionate Christian action to alleviate the drug problems in our own families, schools, and communities.

The discussion that follows focuses on six areas:

1) The American Drug Culture
2) The Great Drug Scare—The Failure of Drug Education
3) Drugs and Family Life
4) Listening
5) Ways to Cope
6) Christian Response—What Can We Do?

THE AMERICAN DRUG CULTURE

We are living in a world filled with drugs. Like all things in this world, they can be used wisely or foolishly. Most of us have used over-the-counter preparations and prescription drugs from time to time without abuse. Some of us have used street drugs. A bottle of aspirin in the medicine cabinet does not constitute a drug menace, yet take a look at all the mood-changing drugs promoted and sold today, and you get a picture of a society that sets a tone for drug experimentation.

First, let's look at the over-the-counter selection. There are pills for every pain: Aspirin, Excedrin, Bufferin, Anacin, Empirin, Tylenol, Datril, Percogesic, Ecotrin, Emagrin, Acription A/D. There are pills to pep us up: NoDoz, Vivarin, Caffedrine. There are pills to calm us down, pills to help us sleep: Nitol, Compōz, Sleep-Eze, Sominex, Quiet World, Nervine, Cope. We have pills to help us lose weight: Thinz-Span, Sip and Slender, Slim-One, Bio-Slim, Sup-Odrinex, Hungrex-plus, Dexatrim, Prolamine. (These contain caffeine and phenylpropanolamine, and are similar to the pep-up pills.) All of these products and more like them are available in a single aisle of your local drug store.

Most of these products, along with our favorite over-the-counter drugs—alcohol and tobacco—are heavily advertised on television, radio, and in magazines and newspapers. Our children are being sold drugs at a very early age. Want to be a real man? Want to be more alluring? Want to relax—or just impress your friends? Or how about getting rid of your tensions at work? Or unwinding from the rowdy kids? Want people to like you? Well, if you believe the advertisements thrust at us day in and day out, we merely have to purchase the right cigarette, the correct wine or beer, or the magic pill. Not everyone who sees an advertisement goes on to become a drug abuser, but they do set a tone: Having trouble coping with life? Try drugs! And not nasty illegal ones, but our friendly, sexy, legal brand names.

Next, let's look at the prescriptions for mood-changing drugs that can be found in many family medicine cabinets. We will discuss only the abusive use of these drugs:

a) Amphetamines (e.g., Benzedrine), Dextro-amphetamine (e.g., Dexedrine), Methamphetamine (e.g., Amphedroxym), Desoxym, Drinalfa, Methedrine, Norodin, Syndrox. You may know these drugs as diet pills. On the drug scene they are "speed," "pep pills," "uppers," "whites."
b) Barbiturates—Amytal, Nembutal, Phenobarbital, Seconal, and Tuinal. These drugs are known as "downers," "reds," "sleeping pills," "sedatives."
c) Nonbarbiturate tranquilizers—Miltown, Equanil, Doriden, Placidyl, Quaalude, Librium, Valium, Thorazine, and Stelazine. These drugs are the most commonly prescribed tranquilizers. While they are not used by youth as frequently as by adults, they are often taken to counter the effects of amphetamines.

These drugs are abused when they are not used as prescribed and monitored by a responsible physician.

Librium and Valium are the most widely prescribed drugs. Because of their widespread availability, many doctors and users have regarded them too casually. Prescriptions are often easy to come by for a user who has become dependent on the tranquilizers. Mixed with alcohol, barbiturates and nonbarbiturate tranquilizers become very dangerous. The most common cases at drug treatment centers are polydrug abuses, and the most common form of polydrug abuse is the combination of pills and alcohol.

Another common abuse of prescription drugs is supplying the drugs knowingly or unknowingly to someone other than the patient for whom it was prescribed. Some of the pills that show up on the streets or in the high schools come from the bottles of diet pills, sleeping pills, and tranquilizers in the family medicine cabinet. We must all be careful of how prescription drugs are used in the home. Be careful to take them as directed. Note when pills are missing, and dispose of leftover pills once they are no longer needed.

Before moving on to the illegal drug market, we must also consider another area where drugs are often legally abused: our schools. Over the years too many of our so-called "problem" children have been placed on sedatives or stimulants on the recommendation of school officials. Children who do not conform to the standards of behavior of a typical classroom are often falsely labeled as "hyperactive," "discipline problems," or "slow learners." Rather than deal with the human problems (which may have as much to do with the schools as with the "problem" children), medical solutions are often imposed. Several hundred thousand children in our elementary schools are receiving drugs so that those schools can cope with them. The most common drug used is Ritalin. Ritalin is an amphetamine. Taken on the streets, we'd call it speed.

The other hallowed area of drug abuse is sports. Drugs are used by athletes, supplied by a trainer or coach, or the athletes may procure the drugs themselves. Drugs used in sports are: mild amphetamines during training to make athletes feel good throughout dull, repetitious practice sessions; anabolic steroids to aid muscle formation; strong amphetamines to psyche them for the actual event; and tranquilizers to help them come down when it's over. Then there are the drugs used to get an athlete to perform despite painful injuries or illness. These drugs include painkillers, tranquilizers, barbiturates, muscle relaxers, anti-inflammants, and enzymes. This use of drugs in sports is most common among professional and college athletes, but their use is not unknown by younger athletes. When big-time sports becomes the most important part of a school, when winning is all-important, we have set an atmosphere for tolerating drug abuse.

Now we move on to the next area of our drug culture—the illegal drug market. Simply *because* of their illegality, it is very difficult to estimate the number of people who have tried or continue to use these drugs. Users are not likely to volunteer information regarding their drug use, so survey findings may be distorted as a result.

Many experts have tried to calculate levels of drug use. *Drug Use Among High School Students 1975–1977*, a study prepared for the National Institute on Drug Abuse by the Institute for Social Research, the University of Michigan, found that 61.6 percent of high school seniors have used illicit drugs at some time. Most of these used only marijuana, but 35.8 percent reported use of illicit drugs other than marijuana.

Lifetime, Annual, and Thirty-Day Prevalence of Use, (and Recency of Use) for Eleven Types of Drugs, Class of 1977

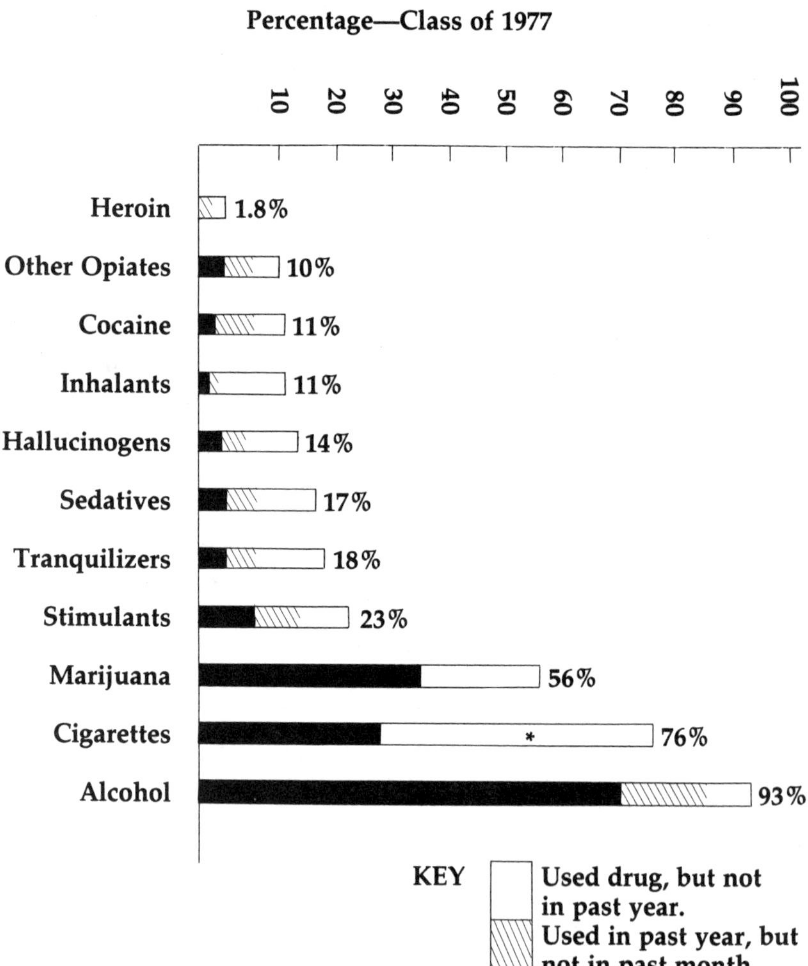

*Annual use was not measured.

SOURCE: Highlights from *Drug Use Among American High School Students 1975–1977.* (University of Michigan), p. 9.

Volumes have been written on the use and effects of various drugs. It would be impossible to give a full presentation on all the drugs that are available on the illegal market. Instead we will briefly identify the most commonly used drugs and refer you to short, simple, and inexpensive guides for more detailed information.

MARIJUANA: The most popular illegal drug is marijuana. The study of high school seniors shows that a majority have tried marijuana and 9.1 percent of them use it daily. Marijuana is a nonaddictive drug that has been illegal in this country since 1937. It has an intoxicating effect and is generally used by youth in much the same manner as adults use alcohol. Most marijuana users fall into the category of recreational users. Studies on health hazards are incomplete but indicate some health problems. These difficulties, however, do not approach the health hazards of alcohol. Many states have lessened the penalties for the possession and use of marijuana, and it is likely that marijuana will be legalized in four to five years. As with Prohibition and alcohol, the illegality of marijuana has not stopped its use, and it has benefited the organized crime rings that control the bulk of imports and sales.

PILLS: The three major categories of pills—amphetamines, barbiturates, and nonbarbiturate tranquilizers—were discussed earlier. Some of the pills on the street market come from family medicine cabinets, many are commercial products that have been diverted to the black market, and others are produced in home labs.

COCAINE: In recent years cocaine has become known as the rich man's recreational drug. Cocaine is a stimulant derived from the coca bush. Its effects are similar to those of amphetamines. It is not considered physically addictive, but it can become a habit. The white powder is usually sniffed through the nostrils. Prolonged use can result in severe irritation of membranes in the nose, sinuses, and throat. The National Institute on Drug Abuse has estimated that eight million Americans have tried cocaine and that one million are current users. Cocaine is expensive, but its use has been growing.

LSD: LSD is the strongest of the hallucinogens. It causes hallucinations and alteration of conscious perception. People who have had traumatic experiences in their youth or who are chronically depressed are more likely than others to have bad experiences with LSD. Flashbacks can also occur following an LSD trip. It is not used as extensively today as it was in the 1960s. LSD use was at its height following the media hype of the San Francisco "Summer of Love" in 1967. LSD is manufactured in home labs and is generally sold in weaker doses now.

PCP: PCP (or "Angel Dust") is an animal tranquilizer with hallucinogenic properties. It has become one of the most popular drugs among youth. PCP was taken in the 1960s by many people who thought they were getting LSD. Today it's being taken by kids who know they're taking PCP. In addition to hallucinations, PCP can have a number of serious, frightening effects. Among them are a feeling of numbness in arms and legs, and symptoms similar to acute schizophrenia and paranoia. PCP has been linked with serious violence. It is taken in capsule form, or is sprinkled on tobacco or marijuana, then smoked.

GLUE AND OTHER INHALANTS: Glue, paint, and aerosols are inhaled to get a high, unfortunately usually by younger children. It's a nasty habit that got widespread publicity in 1959. Ever since, kids have tried to inhale all kinds of products. The vapors are petroleum-based. Use can cause blackouts, anemia, and brain damage.

HEROIN: Heroin (or "smack") is a narcotic derived from the opium poppy. The operation starts with opium poppy farmers in the Far East and Turkey, goes through labs in France, and ends up on the streets in this country after it has been cut with fillers—almost anything that is white and powdery. The entire business is owned and operated by organized crime. After a week or two a user becomes addicted. The high cost and the inability to do much while on the stuff leads many to a life of crime.

Since the 1960s we have seen a different kind of heroin addict. No longer are junkies only poor blacks in the ghetto. Some are, but others are whites from the suburbs. One of the many tragedies of the Vietnam War is the number of men who came home heroin addicts. During the war, the army was appalled by the number of men using marijuana. A full campaign was waged to wipe out marijuana. Then the only available drug was heroin.

Heroin is not a major problem in the high school, but as the high school study showed, there is a small percentage who have used it. High school students looking to buy other illegal drugs often have to deal with people who do have heroin connections, and, as stated before, the heroin business is not run by friendly, spacey hippies. It's a racket and it's run by the folks who do that best.

This is a sampling of some of the drugs that are bought and used illegally. Some are addictive, others are not. Some are more dangerous than others. Using one drug, like marijuana, does not mean that a user will go on to other drugs.

All drugs can be abused regardless of their legal status or method of acquisition. Drugs are abused when they are used in any manner that causes physical, mental, emotional, or social harm to the user or those around him/her. Drug abuse is not limited to the streets. It is not limited to youth.

THE GREAT DRUG SCARE THE FAILURE OF DRUG EDUCATION

It does not take a great deal of study to come to the conclusion that drug education in this country has failed miserably. The most popular theme of drug education has been to "scare the hell out of the kids." Not only has this strategy failed to stop the use of drugs, it has contributed to more widespread use. Incredulous youth have been led to try a new drug just to see if all the wild stories are true. If this seems odd, let's first take a look at a familiar case: the antismoking campaigns.

For centuries, tobacco smokers have known that once they start smoking, they will have difficulty quitting. Smoking was associated with various ills. Since 1964, when the Surgeon General's Report on Smoking and Health was issued, the American public has been continually reminded that the smoke from cigarettes is a primary cause of lung cancer and that the nicotine has an adverse effect on the heart. Smokers will readily acknowledge the health risk they are taking but continue to smoke because of nicotine addiction. We have spent enormous sums of money to publicize the hazards of smoking, and what are the results? Adults have not stopped smoking, and kids have not been dissuaded from starting the habit.

Next horror story: "Marijuana—The Killer Weed!" Marijuana first gained popularity in this country during Prohibition. Up until that time it was used by a small number of musicians and agricultural workers from Mexico. Following the repeal of Prohibition, federal bureaucrats staged a full-scale hysterical campaign against the "evil weed." Hearings were held on how marijuana caused crime, including crazed, violent crimes. Stories were told of murders committed by wild marijuana users who were unable to recall their crimes when confronted. Anyone who has had even the slightest experience with marijuana will recognize the absurdity of these contentions. In fact, a film made in the 1930s to show the evil effects of marijuana—*Reefer Madness*—has become a popular comedy film on college campuses.

Not only does the marijuana campaign backfire on cutting marijuana use, it has called into question the materials presented about other drugs. If some of the stuff we've heard about marijuana is, at best, exaggerated, what about what we hear about speed, PCP, and even heroin? That could be a hoax, too. Well, there is one way to find out—try it. Many, many people have tried new drugs as easily as that.

Drug education has been expensive as well as counterproductive. Besides the obvious exaggerations and errors in drug education efforts, there have been a number of key mistakes made:

a) failing to recognize that drug-taking is part of our culture;
b) identifying the mood-changing drugs themselves as the problem, rather than the personal and cultural problems that lead people to use drugs for a sense of belonging, or self-esteem, or stimulation;

c) not realizing that drug users will continue to use drugs to meet their personal needs unless they are presented with alternatives that also meet those needs.

The drug education effort that focuses on personal needs and feelings rather than pharmaceutical scare tactics is known as primary prevention. Primary prevention focuses on the total health of a community and seeks to deal with an individual's problems *before* they become a drug problem. Emphasis is placed on skills and experiences that get people involved, that give them a feeling of control over their lives and their environment. Doing volunteer work, learning skills like home and auto repair, developing a talent in the arts, pursuing intellectual and spiritual fulfillment, are all ways of meeting our common human needs without drugs. As Christians we are called to create a community that cares about the total development of our brothers and sisters. We were warned not to judge. We are commanded to love one another.

DRUGS AND FAMILY LIFE

Drug use has been the cause of anxiety, pain, fear, and embarrassment in millions of American families. Not understanding drug abuse and reacting to evidence of drug use in hasty judgmental ways has often widened the breach between the drug user and other family members. The immediate reaction is often focused on the evils of the drug in question and the embarrassment the family will suffer if the user is busted, rather than the personal problems that have led the person to experiment with drugs.

We have to recall that drug education begins at home. We cannot expect a few high school assemblies to do the job. Our attitudes about ourselves and about coping with our problems begin at an early age. If parents smoke cigarettes, drink heavily, or abuse other drugs, it will be more difficult to convince children that they should not use drugs. Children with drug-abusing parents are more likely to abuse drugs than other children. At one treatment center in the Northeast, every patient had at least one parent who

was a chronic drug abuser. Unfortunately, actions speak louder than words.

The entire family reacts to a member who has become dependent on drugs. Parents and other children will seek to protect themselves and the family from pain and embarrassment. The immediate goal is to avert any crisis. Parents instinctively try to protect their children from danger. They may cover for a drug-abusing child who faces expulsion from school or loss of a job. Brothers and sisters react to a drug-abusing child in their own way. Some may be protective. Others will keep their distance, particularly if they have been confronted in moralistic tones at home or at school about drugs, whether or not they have shown any indications of drug use. They may resent the brother or sister who has made them an object of undeserved suspicion.

At this point no one in the family is dealing with the reasons *why* a child is using drugs. They are protecting themselves and the user from a crisis. All this does is create an environment where it is easier to use drugs. You can go to school stoned every day confident that Mom and Dad are standing by to bail you out. The family behavior patterns are almost identical to those that develop around an alcoholic parent. (*Note:* This applies to regular and dependent users, not all experimental and recreational users.)

Parents who suspect a drug problem with a child should take some simple steps:

a) **Learn more about drugs being used by youth today.** Youth are much better informed about drugs than their parents. If you attempt to talk about drugs with your children and they sense that you do not know what you are talking about, you will not get too far. Then ask questions.

b) **Maintain good, open relationships with your children.** Create an atmosphere that allows them to share their feelings. Listening is an invaluable skill.

c) **Do not be afraid of a crisis.** If drug abuse has led to dependency, the user may need a crisis to acknowledge his/her dependency on a drug, and the problems it is creating for the user and others at home, school, and work. Avoiding a crisis can perpetuate the problem of drug abuse, and prolong tensions in a family that have led to divorces and estrangement of family members.

d) **Do not be afraid to seek help.** Many local treatment centers, "free clinics," and mental health programs provide support and counseling for families of drug abusers. Al-Anon and Alateen are excellent resources for the families of alcohol abusers, but families and users need different kinds of counseling and support when drugs are involved. The user must admit dependency on a drug and learn to cope with life without drugs. The families have to deal with feelings of guilt, anger, and powerlessness. They must come to grips with the fact that drug users are responsible for their own lives, and that they alone are responsible for the decision to take drugs.

Let's look at a family that learned the hard way. Ed and Laura have been married for twenty-three years. They have a nice home in a suburban community, where they live with their four children: Dan, twenty-one; Jane, nineteen; Bill, seventeen; and Kate, fourteen.

Laura is a housewife with no history of drug abuse. She does not smoke cigarettes and uses alcohol socially. Ed is an engineer. He is a heavy cigarette smoker and a recovered alcoholic. He has been sober for three years. Dan is a pre-med student at a state university. He is an excellent student and does volunteer work at a health clinic near his school. His drug use is limited to occasional recreational use of alcohol and marijuana. Jane is an art student at a small college and has become active in local political campaigns. Her drug experience is also limited to recreational use of marijuana and alcohol. Kate is a freshman at the local high school. She shows no signs of drug experimentation at this point. Bill, a senior at the same school, is a polydrug abuser. On a regular basis he uses tobacco, marijuana, and alcohol. Occasionally he'll use cocaine and speed (amphetamines).

Bill never liked school very much. Despite high I.Q. scores, his grades were usually poor. He did not participate in any school activities and refused to have anything to do with the Church. He hung around kids who felt the same way. Each year the grades got a little worse, the calls home became more frequent. Bill was one of the 15 percent of the students at his high school who went through part of every day high on something.

He became a big shot by helping to arrange drug scores for just about anyone who asked. You could find him most afternoons in the parking lot, cutting classes, getting high. Every few months Laura would get called in to see Bill's guidance counselor. She always assured the school officials that Bill was not a problem at home, and that she and Dan would talk to Bill about his school antics.

The night of one of the parent-guidance counselor sessions, Bill came in at 2:00 A.M. and proceeded to cook his usual bedtime snack—two hamburgers. Ed was waiting for him. He confronted Bill with his bad grades, his poor attendance record, the school's suspicions that he was using drugs on a daily basis and that he might be selling those drugs on school grounds. Bill finished his hamburgers, then yelled at his father, "Well, at least I'm not an alcoholic!"

Not much later Bill was notified that unless he got A's on all his remaining tests and papers, and attended all his classes, he would not be able to graduate with his class. He was sure it was another bluff. He proceeded as usual, and in June he and his embarrassed parents stayed home as their neighbors drove off for the graduation ceremonies. Crisis enough? Oh no.

After summer school, Bill moved out of the house. He was tired of being bothered. He took odd jobs and continued his same habits of drug use. He kept in touch with his high school friends and still sold a small amount of drugs on the side. One night Ed and Laura got a phone call from Bill. He was in jail. The last old buddy to whom he had sold some amphetamines and cocaine had turned him in to the police in order to get the charges dropped in his own case.

That did it. There was just so much Mom and Dad could do now. Laura and Ed arranged for a bail bond, called their lawyer, went home, and painfully sat through the calls from family and friends who had seen the story of Bill's arrest in the newspaper. Years of covering for Bill, schemes to avoid a major crisis—and their worst fears had become a reality anyway. Bill was in jail and the family was on the front page.

Dan and Jane were away at school throughout most of this mess, and they stayed fairly removed from the controversy. Kate got the worst of it. She was given a hard time at school. Kids made cracks about Bill, and school officials were always eyeing her suspiciously. She defended Bill, but she resented him for making life difficult for her.

Bill was convicted of possession and sale of illegal drugs. Because it was a first offense, Bill was fined, placed on probation for four years, and assigned to group counseling at a nearby drug treatment center. Ed and Laura decided to attend the family counseling sessions offered by the treatment center. They are getting help and support from counselors and from others like themselves who know their pain.

LISTENING

Here is what some kids and former kids have to say about drugs.

Ann: I first smoked marijuana in college. I mostly smoked on weekends with friends. I still smoke once in a while, not as much. It's no big deal. I use it the same way I would use alcohol. I've never used any other drugs. I never had any desire to mess with harder drugs.

Sue: I smoked marijuana once in a while during high school. Once I tried some uppers, but I felt so lousy, I'd never do that again. Kids were using all kinds of stuff at my high school—marijuana, lots of speed, acid, some downers, some PCP; cocaine is too expensive for most high school kids, but I did see some. I haven't seen half of that stuff at my college. The high school kids are definitely crazier.

Jim: School is a drag, you know. I have to come here, go to all these classes I don't like. I'm never going to use most of the stuff they're talking about, so what difference does it make if I sit there high? I'm not bothering anybody.

Bob: I really wasted my college years. I was messed up all the time—smoking a lot of grass, dropping acid. One day I realized that I was wasting my life and that I had to regain control of myself. Now I drink beer in moderation and occasionally I'll smoke some grass if it's offered to me at a party. I think most of my friends use grass the same way now. Eventually you get tired of hearing conversations that center around—"how messed up I was last night, how messed up I am now, and how messed up I'm going to be tomorrow."

Ed: Sure I smoke grass. Everybody does. It's not as bad for you as the alcohol my parents drink. One day my mother found some rolling papers and a pipe in my room, and we had a big, screaming fight. Everyone was on my case. But the day Mom got in an accident coming home from a party drunk, no one said anything.

Ray: There's a lot of speed around my school, especially near exam time. There's a lot more Angel Dust showing up, too. I'd never touch that. I saw a kid smoke some Angel Dust and completely flip out. She was going crazy. Some other kids took her to the hospital. Most kids know what they're using and usually stick to pot. Most of the kids use it to party, but there are some kids who get high every day, even in school.

A Drug Counselor: I think kids are more sophisticated about drug use than they were five or ten years ago. I haven't seen as many kids using acid or pills as I used to. PCP seems to be the one exception. Five years ago folks were taking PCP when they thought they had LSD or THC. Now they're taking it for its effects, and *that* I don't understand.

Another Drug Counselor: The most common drug problem I see is polydrug abuse, and it's pills and alcohol. Some of the saddest cases I've ever seen are fifteen- and sixteen-year-old kids that already have brain and liver damage.

The people we see in treatment centers have some points in common. They are frequently the sons and daughters of an alcoholic or other drug abuser. They don't have a good self-image. They have a lot of dependencies and have not learned to accept responsibility for their own actions. They make excuses for everything they do and seek scapegoats in the schools, their families, and their associations.

By the time someone gets to a treatment center, these behavior patterns have been going on for years, and they are much harder to deal with. If I were to give any advice to parents, I'd say, ask questions. Don't be afraid of crisis. Don't insulate yourself from your child's problems. The drug abuser is responsible for the decision to take drugs. You didn't lift the bottle to his mouth or put the needle in his arm. That was not your choice. But don't try to pretend the problems are not there. Like adults, kids take drugs to feel good. The drug itself is not the problem. The real problems are the reasons why the person takes drugs.

High School Principal: It's very difficult for me to get an accurate picture of the extent of drug use at our school. People have told me that we have a problem here. So I say O.K., give me some information, some names. But I never get anything. It's the great unknown. I'm not naive enough to think we don't have a problem, but it's difficult to get more than a good feeling for it.

For the most part we see marijuana and alcohol use. Lowering the drinking age to eighteen in this state has made alcohol more available to fourteen- and fifteen-year-olds—beer and hard liquor. A couple of years ago we had students apprehended in school and in the community, but that has not happened to us in the last few years.

I don't think students are coming to class stoned. Of course that can be hard to tell. Some teachers don't notice if a student is high, and some are so hyper about drug use that they think a student is on something when it may only be a lack of sleep, or a cold.

My experience with kids that have gotten into trouble with drugs is that their self-image is poor. I have particularly noticed the absence of a father—physical and spiritual. I don't mean cases where the father is absent because of divorce or death. I mean cases where the father's role in the family is limited to providing a paycheck.

If I were to give any advice to parents who are concerned that their kids are using drugs or might be using drugs, I'd tell them to first be willing to face the problem.

I'm amazed at how blind parents can be. High school is a little late in the game, but something can be done.

Recognize that your kid has a problem and stop blaming it on a peer group. If you talk to parents of the peer group, you'll find they're blaming your kid. There is an unwillingness to accept responsibility for our own actions and the schools are a favorite whipping boy.

Being a parent is an awesome task. Don't lose a child by default. The schools and parents have to cooperate. If we continue to blame each other, nothing gets done.

COPING WITH DRUG USE

"An ounce of prevention is worth a pound of cure." That old maxim holds true for drug abuse. Good primary education is certainly a more attractive alternative than the alternatives to be considered after the fact of drug abuse. For some drug users, primary prevention principles can still be used to avoid regular and dependent use of drugs. For others, additional therapy will be required.

Sooner or later all families have to face the fact that their children are going to be exposed to drugs (alcohol, tobacco, and illegal drugs) in college and high school, if not in junior high school. A vast majority of them are going to try tobacco, alcohol, and marijuana. Many of them are going to try other drugs.

Parental concerns generally focus on the effects of drug use on physical health and personal development, and on the illegality of using certain drugs. All of these are legitimate concerns. Discussions on these topics are controversial. Let's look at the health effects first.

Any drug that we take, be it penicillin, aspirin, tobacco, alcohol, marijuana, or heroin, has some effect on the body other than the effect for which it is taken. Drugs that can cure our ills and stop our pains have side effects that harm us in some way. This certainly holds true for all the mood-changing drugs mentioned here. Some drugs are more harmful than others. Very often in the case of illegal drugs, not enough is known about the effects of their use. Their very illegal status has impeded research. If you are concerned about the effects of a particular drug, do some research. And remember—drugs do not have to be illegal to be harmful.

Can drugs impede personal development? Anything that is used to blot out the real world on a regular basis can affect anyone's ability to grow as a person. A person who is almost always under the influence of a drug is going to have a harder time developing a healthy sexual identity, vocational direction, healthy interpersonal relations, and an overall sense of personal worth than someone who tries to face life with all its growing pains without relying continually on drugs. Someone who smokes marijuana recreationally may experience no unusual difficulty in coping with life. However, adolescents or adults who continually attempt to function in school, or at work, or at home while under the influence of a drug are telling us that they do not have the strength or confidence to deal with the problems and conflicts in their lives. Drug abuse is not just an impediment to further personal growth. It is a warning signal that real personal problems already exist.

The matter of the legal status of drugs is a much debated topic. In recent years we have seen moves to lessen the penalties for possession of marijuana in many states. There are groups working for the legalization of marijuana on the grounds that it is not as harmful as other drugs that are legally available; its use is widespread and growing despite prohibition; its present status provides a bonanza for organized crime; its use is a matter of personal choice and does not make anyone a criminal.

Still other people advocate the legalization of all drugs in order to remove the criminal aspect of drug use and deal with the reasons why the user is involved with drugs. Advocates of decriminalization are not advocating drug use but argue that the drug laws in this country have not stopped the use of illegal substances, and that some laws seem to violate the Eighth Amendment's prohibition of cruel and unusual punishment. Opponents feel that enough damage is caused by alcohol and tobacco, and that it would be unwise to make other drugs available legally.

Regardless of how you feel about the legal status of marijuana, and other illegal drugs, the fact remains that its sale, possession, and use are still against the law. The penalties for possession of illegal drugs vary from state to state. Depending on where you live, you may be facing a misdemeanor charge and a small fine, or a jail sentence for possession of marijuana for personal use. Be familiar with the drug laws in your state. If the laws seem unfair to you, remember that laws can be changed. Discuss the laws with your children. The courts are filled with people who never thought they would be caught.

Where can parents go for help with a drug problem? Informed, calm parents can often discuss drug use with experimental and recreational users of drugs. The discussions require mutual respect and sharing of feelings. An objective third party may help facilitate discussion. In the end, only the user controls the decision to smoke, drink, or take other drugs, but you can share your concerns openly and honestly.

Regular drug users may react favorably to discussions moderated by a third party but will often require additional therapy to intervene in drug use that may be approaching dependency. Help cannot be imposed. The drug user must recognize the need for help.

Dependent users need outside help to get off drugs and learn ways of coping with life without chemical aids. Alcoholics Anonymous is an excellent resource for people who have a problem with alcohol alone, or with alcohol combined with other drugs. Unfortunately, there is no comparable group for handling other drug abuses on a national scale.

Drug treatment programs vary from community to community. In some areas there will be a number of programs with different philosophies and different treatment techniques. If you are looking for help, and you are living in an area that has different alternatives, check them out. Visit centers and talk to the staffs. Then, together with the drug user, decide which program best meets the drug user's needs.

The person seeking therapy should make the final decision, if possible, to enter a treatment program. (Many patients did not volunteer for treatment but were arrested for a drug-related offense and given the choice of jail or treatment. Others may have been pressured by an employer to seek help or lose their jobs.) Remember that drug users are responsible for their decisions to take drugs. They must acknowledge their problem with drugs and be willing to seek help. As a parent you may want a child to get off drugs, but until that child accepts the need for help, no treatment can succeed.

A family develops its own problems and anxieties when a member of the family abuses drugs. Whether or not a drug abuser seeks treatment, family members can get help and support to deal with the problems in their own lives that arise because of drug abuse.

SUGGESTIONS FOR FURTHER ACTION

HOME:

- Set an example for responsible use of all drugs.
- Share *accurate* information on drugs with your children.
- Create an atmosphere for sharing feelings before real trouble develops.
- Encourage talents and interests that develop confidence, personal awareness and healthy interpersonal relationships.

SCHOOL:

- Keep lines of communication open with your child's principal, teachers, and advisors.
- Work with other concerned parents and school staff to develop and/or evaluate better drug education programs. (Remember that drug education should begin at home long before a child reaches high school.)

TREATMENT CENTERS:

- Become familiar with drug treatment and counseling programs in your area. Get to know the people running the programs. Many communities have inadequate or no facilities for detoxification and treatment of women with children. Make sure your community has facilities adequate to its needs.

PARISH:

• Sponsor forums, discussion sessions. Avoid the school assembly format. Don't use a speaker onstage with adjournment following the speech. Try informal sessions with your school principal or a drug counselor that will allow everyone to participate in the discussion.

• Use the parish communication system to publicize drug information events, the names and phone numbers of drug treatment and counseling centers in your area, and the names and addresses of groups that publish drug information materials for parents and youth.

• Preach about drug use and alternatives. Don't back off from a concern of many parishioners.

• Examine your youth ministry. Are you reaching all the youth in your area or just a segment? Realize that a lot of youth who turn to drugs are turned off by institutional churches. Many will respond to the tradition of mysticism or social justice programs, as well as social activities. *Talk to the youth.* Find out what kind of activities they would like to see in the parish.

• Examine the drug laws in your state. Compare them with laws in other states, and decide whether or not your laws are consistent with Christian principles of social justice. If they are not, join with other concerned people in your parish, your diocese, and your state to lobby for change in the laws.

REGINA M. RYAN. Ms. Ryan holds a B.A. in Political Science from LeMoyne College. She is a community organizer and freelance writer.

THE SINGLE-PARENT FAMILY: SCOPE AND NATURE

Kathleen Kircher

In recent years, the American Catholic Community, much like American society in general, has been alerted to rapid changes taking place within the family structure. One area of widespread concern and interest is that of the single-parent family.

The commonly held notion that the American Catholic community is extensively composed of nuclear families, modeled on age-old descriptions of the Holy Family, is painfully crumbling. In recent years, sociologists have carefully sketched the emerging faces of alternate family lifestyles gaining recognition within our social backdrop of "primary groupings." The term "family" has undergone the assault of many who sense the timeliness of enlarging its definition and usage to match the developing alternate familylike structures.

Today the prevalence of single-parent families is expanding rapidly. Dr. Paul C. Glick, Senior Demographer in the Population Division of the Census Bureau, states that the total number of children under eighteen years of age in 1977 is about the same as the total population of children in 1960. While we experience this overall sameness in numbers of children, Dr. Glick points out that the total number of children living with a single parent has doubled, the number living with a divorced parent has tripled, and the number living with a never-married parent has increased by 700 percent.

While it may be difficult, if not impossible, to keep up with such rapidly changing statistics, their implications clearly resound: the single-parent family is a growing part of American society. And since we know that the American

Catholic community is no longer immune from societal changes, we must examine our structures and determine their availability and usefulness to the single-parent family. It is, indeed, comfortable and praiseworthy to continue to meet needs of nuclear families. The question of responding to disparate groups, which have at least equal need for assistance and support, is another matter.

The term "single-parent family" refers simply to those homes in which there is one parent rather than two. Today many reasons account for single-parent families—death, separation, divorce, adoption, unmarried parenting, imprisonment. The astounding increase in single-parent families is obviously affected by a variety of causes, but today there prevails a shift toward the belief that becoming a single parent is easier to achieve and often advisable.

Reversed attitudes toward single parenting have not dramatically reduced the unique problems experienced by members of single-parent families in our parishes or neighborhoods. It is not as easy for one parent to raise children alone as it is when two parents cooperate.

Whenever we consider singleness and parenting, we uncover a dual challenge. Single parents often need helpful support in understanding and maintaining the balance between their own need for personal growth and development and their responsibility for the care of their children. The most well-adjusted single parent can be guilt-ridden from time to time whenever the balance between self-centered and child-centered decisions is skewed. The most dedicated and selfless parent can feel deep resentment or hostility toward his/her children when their needs and company become all-consuming. Certainly, what is intensified in the single-parent family are the additional responsibilities of confronting problems alone and, ultimately, resolving them through decision-making devoid of beneficial discussions with an intimately involved other person.

More than 90 percent of children under eighteen, within the single-parent family, live with the mother. Considering single-parent families with children under six years of age, some 96 percent of these households are headed by the mother or another significant female, such as a grandmother or an aunt.

It is imperative, therefore, that we focus on female head-of-households in our attempt to respond helpfully. Dr. Alice Cook of Cornell University has studied working mothers' roles and responsibilities in nine countries. She has concluded that working mothers spend only slightly fewer hours at housekeeping than do professional homemakers. Some four to eight hours a day are spent by working mothers on household tasks. We may well wonder how they manage, especially as single parents! Dr. Cook found their solution to be careful budgeting of every hour and—for some—only six hours of sleep.

Within our society today, available day care services seem to be embarrassing, inadequate, or inaccessible. Gladys Gardner Jenkins, a lecturer in single parenting, reports that the cost per child for a minimum day care center is approximately $1200 per year, and that a desirable program approaches $2300. If we are impelled to support single parents who choose family togetherness, we must seek alternate services for parents who cannot afford such fees.

Dr. Cook, in this recent study, discovered innovative approaches to child care needs. Can we, with careful planning and determined interest, adapt or adopt some of these relief measures? Dr. Cook learned that:

(1) Sweden developed day care centers where children can report after school; these also provided caretakers for sick children enrolled in the programs so that adequate home care could be maintained throughout the child's sickness;
(2) Scandinavian countries hire park-mothers to insure adequate outdoor exercise for children;
(3) Israel offers full-day schools where parents can request afternoon activities, supervised study, and outdoor recreational activity for their children;
(4) Japan establishes day care centers on a population-ratio basis within each city ward.

As we learn of the scarcity of day care services within our neighborhood, the challenge to respond escalates. Recently, however, some parish-based day care services are developing, particularly in inner-city areas but also in rural villages.

Family and pastoral counselors often highlight the plight of loneliness that constantly surfaces among most single parents. The mere fact that one is not "one-half" of a couple diminishes social interaction. Segregation of single persons, both subtle and implicit from church/community events is widespread. Despite this couple-oriented milieu, many single parents refuse to see themselves as social misfits. Dr. Kathleen Monaghan Leckband, sociology professor at Marymount Manhattan College in New York, learned that single parents are adapting to single-parent status by forming community connections with other single parents or with those in mixed marital status. In her interviews some sixty single parents spoke of their determination to extend themselves into the community rather than isolate themselves. Support groups for those in like circumstances can be extremely helpful, especially during transition periods when one is learning new ways to cope with traumatic events such as death, divorce, separation. When the need for a support group lessens, however, the recovering person seeks inclusion within the broader community. Can we mature to the point where we can enjoy one another as persons, rather than pairs?

Throughout this discussion of being a single person and parent, there exists a danger to stereotype all single-parent families as if they experience identical characteristics and needs. This dangerous tendency has certainly been prevalent whenever we discuss the needs of people in other areas, such as the handicapped or the aged. Therefore, we should explicitly state that church/civic responses to the single-parent family must focus on the individual family and not on the group.

There is a real difference in needs between the older, competent parent seeking day care services during school vacations and the unmarried teen-age parent who forms a family with her young child. Strong differences exist between single parents of adolescents and those of primary school-age children. This is especially true whenever the parent's need for an intimate social life disturbs the adolescent son/daughter. The varied causes of becoming a single parent, scattered decision-making abilities, familial and financial pressures—each factor effects the self-esteem and competency of each single parent.

For most of us, shedding stereotypic myths about families that differ from the so-called "normal home" is painfully difficult. Research is more strongly indicating that the health of the parent/child family lies within the quality of parenting, not within the family structure. Two-parent families may be inadequate in parenting; single-parent families can be viable when the parent competently provides a warm, loving, support community.

Those who employ such labels as the "normal home" frequently refer to certain single-parent families as the "broken home." This connotation is also a myth. Single-parent homes are not broken homes. The single-parent home often differs from the first home in that tense arguments cease. The home that was broken, therefore, no longer continues. Those caught in the error of "broken home" thinking often speak offhandedly and caustically to children within the single-parent family. Frequently, family members, aware of an impending second marriage, remark to children: "Soon you're going to be part of a real family again." How often we forget that single-parent families *are* real families.

Closely aligned to these mistaken notions is the erroneous belief that children from one-parent families are delinquent, problem children. Researchers, like Dr. Morton Hunt and Dr. Michael Rutter, strongly denounce the broken home theory as the major cause for delinquent behavior. Their findings indicate that the harmful effects of discord, tension, and argument have far more serious effects upon children's behavior than the actual parental separation. While it remains true that a larger percentage of male delinquent children come from divorced families. Dr. Rutter concludes that the patterns of behavior learned in the discordant home before the parental separation rather than the fact of single-parent family status correlate with later delinquent action more significantly.

The commonly held assumption that fathers cannot be as competent as mothers in parenting qualities is another myth slowly being dispelled. Parenting programs for fathers who parent because of adoption, death, or child custody decisions are proving to be successful. Sometimes these programs need to be coupled with temporary homemaker services to permit adequate male preparation for the art of parenting. Such compassionate considerations, especially in sudden losses such as the death of the mother, can express our confidence that fathers, as well as mothers, can be adept at parenting.

Lastly, we must be aware that some 80 percent of single-parent families will become a blended family due to second marriage. Some of the difficulties inherent in this merger are reflected by the conflicting loyalties experienced by the children. Comparisons, jealousies, overwhelming adjustments to stepparents and extended family members can be extremely difficult and confusing. Support services offered to single-parent families must consider its usually transitional status and include challenging and insightful assistance preparatory to a second marriage.

There remain unanswered questions concerning the welfare of children in single-parent families. Further knowledge and research are needed in these areas:

(1) To explain why some children remain more vulnerable to the effects of a broken home.

(2) To determine whether children need two-sex parenting in order to develop their biological sexual identity; and, if so, how this can be provided for at different age levels within the single-parent home.

(3) To delineate the response of boys and girls to the lack of a father figure, typical of some 90 percent of the single-parent families.

Within this essay, recent and pertinent data related to the single-parent family—its scope and nature—has been summarized. The expected result includes the challenge to examine our parish/church structures in order to evaluate their ministerial effectiveness with the growing single-parent community. Each of us can be more aware of spotting the child who is at risk following a break in the nuclear family group. All of us can stretch our understanding of the needs of the single person and parent as we consider the conditions under which the family is functioning. As Christian community, we are called to service of others. Single-parent families, seeking inclusion rather than exclusion, affirmation rather than negation, propel us into Christian response and service.

SUGGESTIONS FOR FURTHER ACTION

Suggested courses of assistance to single parents that can be requested by parish/civic task forces concerned with the single-parent family include:

(1) High school programs for teen-age mothers, before and after childbirth; also, programs acclimated to the development of parenting skills for the teen-age father;

(2) programs sponsored by counseling agencies that focus on the needs and problems of children, particularly those traumatized by the breaking apart of a double-parent family through death or divorce;

(3) family counseling programs for parent and child/children in order to think through the meaning of a divorce or loss of a parent for some other reason;

(4) programs sponsored by and inclusive of family court and legal systems that examine and articulate children's legal rights so that greater emphasis can be placed on the child's preference to live with the parent to whom the child is more strongly attached;

(5) programs sponsored by children's librarians within public library systems that include books and films for children in single-parent families.

KATHLEEN KIRCHER, S.S.J. Sister Kathleen has a master's degree in Counseling from Boston College. She is the Director of Ministry to Divorced, Separated and Remarried Catholics in the Diocese of Rochester, and is also on the Advisory Board of the North American Conference of Separated and Divorced Catholics.

THE ORDEAL OF THE POOR IN AMERICA

Cosmo F. Ferrara

Today Americans are swirling in a spiral of inflation. It may be the wrong time to ask a family that is struggling to pay its own bills to consider for a moment those "less fortunate."

"I have enough of my own problems," would seem to be a fair response from people who, even with a salary increase, are losing money every year.

Though we fret over the car payments, scrimp and save for the kids' tuition, cut vacations short or out completely, introduce the family to meatless menus, we Christians cannot ignore the poor.

"The poor? That's me, isn't it?"

Perhaps you do fall within the government's guidelines of "poor." Perhaps you are among the 25 million Americans who suffer from a lack of adequate food, housing, clothing, medical care and other necessities. Perhaps you are among the 10 million Americans who go to bed hungry every night. Maybe you do try to prepare meals for your family of four on $1.41 a day per person; and pay the rent with $150 a month; and cover the costs of medical and dental care, personal and property insurance, clothing, furniture, and home repair, utilities, transportation, school expenses, taxes, cultural activities, entertainment, and everything else on about $48 a month per person.

These figures are drawn from the latest government studies that peg the poverty cutoff at $6,191 for a family of four. This means that a family of four with a total yearly income under $6,191 is considered "poor." For a person living alone the figure is $3000; for a couple it is about $4000.

At the same time the poor are going hungry, they are watching other Americans feed 25 percent of the world's tuna catch to their pets and spend over $5 billion a year on cosmetics and diet products. While they wait hours at a clinic to see a doctor, more than 15 million of their fellow citizens are plunking down about $10 each for pro football tickets every year. As an aged neighbor limps to the drug store for his medicine, more than half a million people in the United States are buying new cars each month. While families across the nation watch television shows featuring split-level homes, exquisite clothes, and exciting toys, the poor family watches the *same shows*—knowing they cannot have any of these fine things.

The effects of these hardships and contrasts can be seen in the report of a thirty-three-year-old man found hanged in his apartment. He was apparently despondent over not being able to find a job, and unemployment compensation was exhausted. His wife and four children left him and had returned to Mississippi where they had emigrated from seven years ago. The family had been several months arrears in rent, and there was not proper food and clothing for the family during the harsh winter months.

Many of our fellow Americans—more than 25 million of them—are this poor, though we may not see them. And chances are we will not see them unless we travel the back roads of Appalachia, venture into the blighted streets of the cities, visit the lonely old people in heatless apartments, suffer the stench of the nation's skid rows. We won't see the poor at meetings of unions, social clubs, and political parties because the poor do not belong. We won't see them on television because the poor are not attractive. We won't see them where we work, shop, eat; where we dance, study, laugh.

To most of us the poor are invisible, but they exist in frightening numbers and dreary settings.

Louise W——, age seventy-three, lives by herself in a single furnished room on the third floor of a rooming house located in a substandard section of the city. In this one room, she cooks, eats, and sleeps. She shares a bathroom with other lodgers. Widowed at sixty-four, she has few friends remaining from her younger years. Those who do remain do not live near her, and it is difficult for her to see them. Louise stays confined to her one room and the bathroom shared by nine other people. When the weather is warm enough, she ventures down the long flight of stairs about once a week for a walk to the corner and back.

Of all the Americans living below the threshold of poverty, close to 4 million of them are elderly, mostly single people trying to live on about $2900 a year. At an age when medical care and supplies are needed more, these people can afford them even less. There is nothing graceful and dignified about growing old in a society that cherishes youth, vitality, and good health, when you are old and cannot afford the food and medical care you need; or lack the transportation or strength to go shopping; or won't step out of your tiny apartment for fear of being beaten and robbed.

Yet the general attitude of our country toward the elderly is often one of impatience, resentment, and neglect. Television tells us the aged are either senile, cranky, or constipated. The decline of neighborhoods with strong familial ties has eroded social means by which older persons were supported and cared for.

At the other end of the spectrum are the children who are poor, about 10 million of them in this country. Nowhere is the cycle of poverty more chilling and deadly than among children. Young people who lack the opportunities to decent health, nourishment, housing, schooling and stable family life are starting out with enormous odds against them. They must live among rats, roaches, crime, drugs, and violence. They are hungry, and poor health follows them all their lives, perpetuating itself. A young child's nutritional deficiencies result in mental and physical problems that could take three generations of good health to offset.

Many poor adolescents quit school early to help bring some money home, thereby eliminating all chance of their learning skills that will carry them into the mainstream of economic survival in America.

The greatest tragedy of all, though, is the potential that is wasted as the minds and spirits of these children quickly begin to deteriorate and rot.

Michael Harrington writes of poor children in an area of St. Louis, Missouri. His clients were, for the most part, children of transient Arkansas sharecroppers and cotton pickers.

The houses these people lived in had probably been the homes of aristocrats of an earlier day, which had now been cut into many rooms and packed with families. Generally, there were no working bathrooms inside these places. There were outhouses in the back yards, sometimes near the common pump.

The children were forced to go to school under state law, but it was a battle to get them there. In the eighth grade, sixteen was the average age. The school made showers and hair checks compulsory, but these measures could not compete with homes that were dirty, rat-infested, and bug-ridden.

There were families who could not send their children to school because there were not enough shoes to go around. One family passed the shoes from child to child, so that at least a couple of them would be in school each day. Many had such low I.Q.'s that any attempt at standard education would fail. Teachers had difficulty teaching them the rudiments of living, such as understanding traffic lights and distinguishing money.

"One of the most frustrating things about social work," Harrington concludes, "is that one could read the fates written on some of the children's faces. It was relatively easy to guess which boys might end up in a penitentiary, which girls would become pregnant before they were out of grade school."

Between the children and the elderly are the working poor. Sixty percent of all the poor in America—about 15 million men and women—work either part-time or full-time, yet never escape being the "have-nots" of society. Working full-time every week of the year and earning the legal minimum wage, a person will still fall below the poverty line.

The psychological despair that is conditioned into people who work full-time yet never get ahead—or even close to catching up—is one of the most devastating effects of poverty.

Many Americans, however, find it hard to believe that anyone who is able and willing to work could still be poor. Many believe that welfare recipients are lazy loafers, able-bodied moochers freeloading off the rest of society. The fact of the matter is that two-thirds of the people living below the poverty line receive no welfare at all. Either because they are not aware of the help that is available to them, or because they cannot master the maze of registration procedures, or have no way of getting to the welfare offices, most of America's poor do not receive the aid for which they are eligible.

Of those poor who receive aid, 75 percent are children, elderly, disabled, or blind. Many of the remaining adult recipients who may be capable of working are single parents with children who need tending. So the "lazy loafer" label hardly applies to the poor.

Another myth about welfare is that people get rich on it. But the fact is that not one state grants welfare payments equal to the federal government's poverty threshold, which we have seen is very low. Anyone forsaking work to collect welfare is destined to remain poor.

"But they are making money elsewhere and still collecting from government programs," some people argue. "Most people on welfare are cheats."

Misallocation of welfare monies amounts to only about 4 percent of the annual expenses for these programs. The percentage of error is lower here than in federal income tax calculations. In one year, for example, tax experts estimate that one-third of the nation's taxpayers underreported about $30 billion of taxable income, with an estimated loss of about $6 billion in revenues to the government. Needless to say, most of these people were living well above the subsistence level.

Yet the American public seems to soft-pedal or accept tax delinquents, while at the same time coming down hard on welfare recipients, considering all of them frauds. One who looks objectively at the facts, though, sees that people on welfare are the rejects, very much in need of the aid they receive. Still, public reaction is to punish.

To blame the poor for being poor is a dodge, a rationalization to ease our consciences and to perpetuate a grossly uneven distribution of the blessings God has bestowed on America. To say that the poor do not share the fruits of our

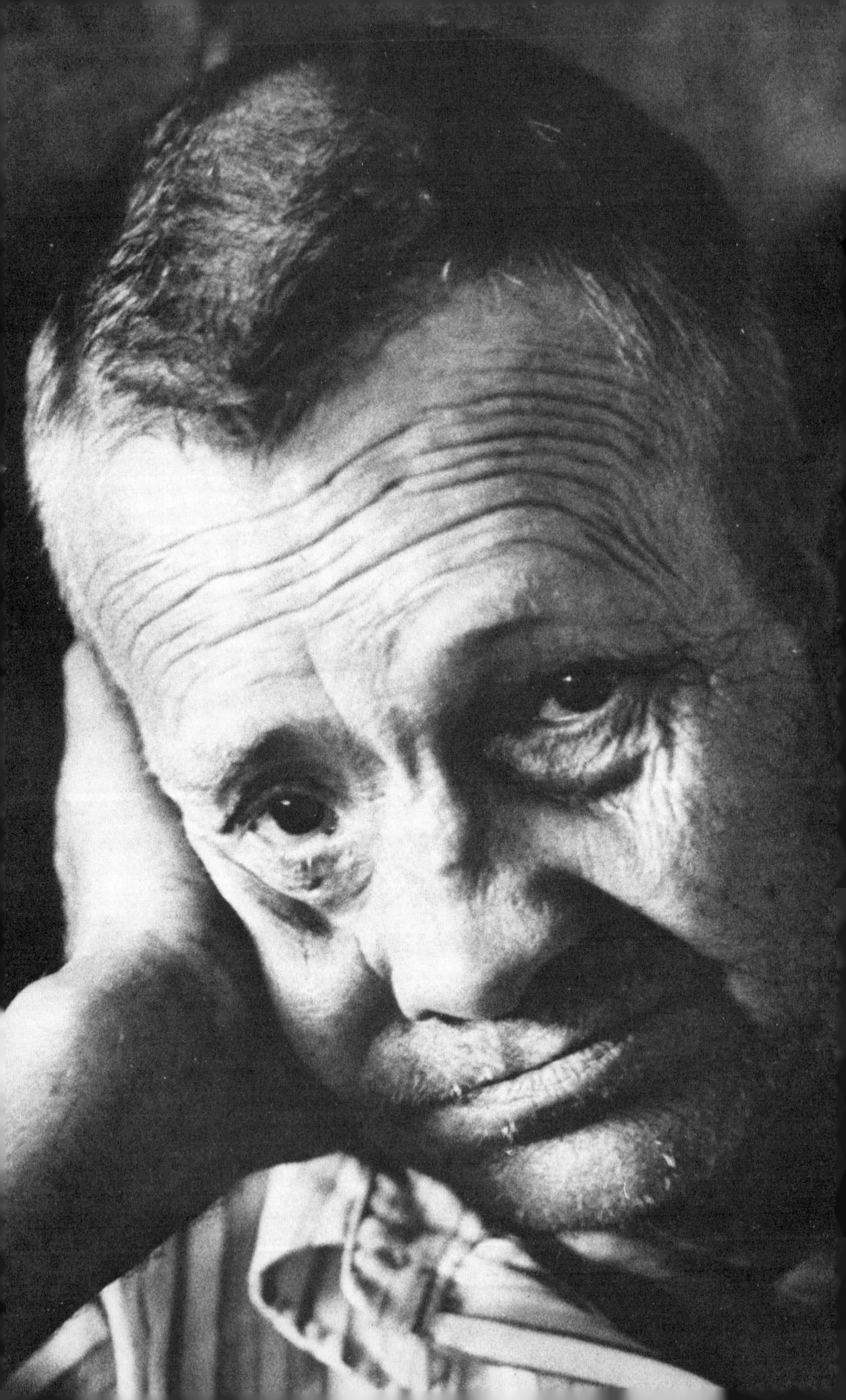

society because they are "not in tune" with its workings, because they only "live for today," or are "poor but happy," released from the tensions of the middle-class world, is to ignore the realities of research and observation.

Studies have shown that there are three times as many psychiatric cases found among the poor than among any other class of Americans. The reasons seem to be the number of "stress factors" gnawing at the poor. In childhood the poor experience the bad mental and physical health of their parents, economic deprivation, quarrelsome and broken homes, negative attitudes toward parents. In adult life, their own bad health and inadequate medical care, work worries, marital worries, parental worries, money worries, and a lack of friends and real companions build up a barrage of stress factors difficult to resist. To consider the poor somehow "heartier" and better able to deal with their sad lot is contrary to fact and reason.

If anything, today's poor are less able than their counterparts of generations ago. These are not the adventurous spirits seeking a new land and new life. No, most of today's poor are the offspring of the poor, or the failures, driven from the land and bewildered by the city, old people suddenly confronted by loneliness and squalor, workers made obsolete by technology, minorities facing a world of prejudice. They own nothing, dream nothing, and though huddled in tenements or shanties, they belong to no one and no thing.

So rather than a heartiness, there is a hopelessness and helplessness, an inability to climb out of the slimy pit alone. Without good nutrition and medical care, without quality education, without access to assistance programs and work opportunities, without skills and quality education, the poor are battling the dragon with a papier-mâché sword.

Those who care, then, must work to equalize the odds. Instead of blaming the victim, we must focus attention on the villain, not on the symptoms but on the causes, not on motivation but on opportunity.

As individuals and groups we can shop for the old man down the street, help the unwed mother fill out the welfare forms, get those sickly children washed and cared for, train those men and women for decent jobs, and put them in contact with the people who can hire them.

And we help without condescension but with a spirit of Christian charity and obligation. "I was hungry and you gave me food . . . . As you did it to one of the least of these my brethren, you did it to me . . . . As you did it not to one of the least of these, you did it not to me" (Matt. 25:35–45).

Our personal compassion must be accompanied by group efforts to work within and, in some cases, to change the structures of society. As voting members of a democracy, we use our political rights to have legislation enacted that will make aid accessible to those who need it most, and to break down further the walls of prejudice and inequality that are the mainstays of poverty. As consumers we can wield an economic clout in the private sector to end exploitation of the poor and open opportunities to them.

To erase poverty in America is a dream that can be realized, but only if broad changes are made in the structures of society and sincere changes made deep in the hearts of each of us. In the story of the rich man and Lazarus, Jesus does not say the rich man exploited Lazarus, but yet He criticizes the man's lack of concern for the sick beggar lying outside his gate. "Clothed in purple and fine linen," the rich man "feasted sumptuously every day." Lazarus desired to be fed "with what fell from the rich man's table" (Luke 16:19–31). Did the rich man deny the beggar those scraps? Probably not. Did he go out of his way to make life miserable for Lazarus? No. Yet Christ was not pleased with him. He expected more than refraining from exploitation and offering scraps. He expected concern in the form of positive action. Though we may not "feast sumptuously" or be "clothed in purple," though we do not exploit, and though we do assist welfare programs through our taxes, Christ seems to expect more from his followers. "Let us not live in word or speech, but in deed and truth" (John 3:17–18).

Who Are Today's Poor?

AGE: Mostly children, elderly

	Number	*% of all poor*
Under age 18	10,028,000	41%
Aged 18–64	11,515,000	46%
Over age 64	3,177,000	13%

HOME: More in central cities, rural areas

	Number	*% of all poor*
In central cities	9,203,000	38%
In suburbs	5,657,000	22%
Outside metropolitan areas	9,861,000	40%

REGION: Largest number in South

	Number	*% of all poor*
South	10,249,000	41%
West and North	14,471,000	49%

RACE: Whites, 2 out of 3

	Number	*% of all poor*
White	16,416,000	61%
Black*	7,726,000	29%
Hispanic	2,700,000	10%

SOME MYTHS AND FACTS ABOUT WELFARE

MYTH: Welfare recipients are lazy loafers
FACT: 94% of all able-bodied, adult recipients work
MYTH: All welfare recipients are black
FACT: More than half of the welfare recipients are not black*
MYTH: Welfare recipients breed many children and thus collect continuously more money
FACT: The average number of children in a family receiving welfare is 2.6 children
MYTH: Most welfare recipients cheat
FACT: Misallocation of funds totals only 4% of annual expenses, a lower percentage than error in federal income tax calculations

*1 of every 3 blacks is poor

POVERTY AND FAMILY LIFE

Cosmo F. Ferrara

"Home life is the highest and finest product of civilization. It is the great molding force of mind and of character. Children should not be deprived of it except for urgent and compelling reasons." So declared the White House Conference on Children in 1909.

Today, some 10 million American children in poverty-stricken families are being deprived of childhood as a specially prolonged and protected stage in the life cycle. They experience instead hunger, illness, depravity, crime, early initiation into sex, free unions and consentual marriages, a high incidence of abandonment, female-dominated homes, a lack of privacy, a surplus of sibling rivalry, and competition for goods and affection.

One caseworker in New York described one such home: "In this six-story building, converted into furnished rooms, filth prevails throughout. Filled garbage cans without covers line the hallways with the surplus refuse spilling over; roaches and rats abound; broken flooring, plumbing, windows, lighting fixtures, and plaster are observable throughout. The average room-size occupied by a family is 13′ by 15′, with two beds, a dresser, two chairs, a table, a refrigerator, and a closet. One community kitchen is used by seven families. Twelve toilets are intermittently in service on six floors. There is no lock on the door from the street, and vagrants, including drug addicts and alcoholics, often wander in to sleep in the halls, the unlocked kitchens, or bathrooms. This is the abode of 30 families and 105 children."

The children are very much aware of the misery in which they live. This sixth grader, whose writing is typical of the poor education these children receive, is nonetheless clear on the squalor around his home. "I am not satifeyed with the dope addictes around our block. They take dope in our hallway every night. Another is they break in stores and bars. I am desatified with the lady that live under us. She set fire to Doris's door. Some dope backs live under us. The lady under us robbed Teddy's aunt for $17.00's. One night a dope addict went crazy in our hally way. They are so many bums in our block. Please help to get and keep them out."

In studying poverty one finds a number of causes. Racial prejudice is still a primary cause, with one out of every three blacks being poor. Old age, disabilities, and technological changes keep many people out of work and poor. Little education and serious illness are still other causes. Often these become the effects of one generation's poverty and the causes of a second generation's. One of the fallacies in the land of opportunity is that most of the people who die poor were born poor.

Taking a close look at the way the poor live can tell us a good deal about why they live that way. To know of both is the first step in trying to eliminate poverty.

Those who study the poor find certain patterns or stages in the lives of the poor and draw conclusions that should be a help in combatting poverty. The four stages are these: 1) the timing and circumstances of the first marriage and first childbearing; 2) the timing and direction of occupational choices; 3) the family cycle squeeze, creating a conflict between aspiration and need; and 4) the family breakdown.

Looking at these four stages, we see a multiplicity of factors coming together keeping the poor where they are. In Stage 1, those who marry young and who have children early, and who have many children, increase their chances of being poor significantly. These are people who have less education, find less work, and make less money to spend on larger families. Only one-half of the women married at age seventeen will be living with the same husband thirty years later. Yet half the women married at seventeen have four children. The strain on the marriage is obvious, often leading to separation. The income problem is a source of reinfection for each new marriage, and each new marital failure is likely to add to the income problem.

One mother of ten children differed with her husband over what to do with their pregnant, unwed daughter. In explaining her position she sheds light on the cycle of early childbearing that keeps many poor people in their dire predicament. "I told him she ain't the first one who ever made a mistake, and I was going to let her stay right here with me. I told Esther we would take care of her through this one, but no more babies before you're married. I did this because I had made a mistake and got pregnant, and I could understand how anybody could make a mistake at least once."

Many of these "mistakes" occur as a result of the ignorance about sex typical among the poor. One woman said "My mother told me about 'ministrating.' She never told me about sex, nothing about a man, and she say—after I got up the nerve to ask her—'you fool around with a boy, you get a baby' and that was all."

As hard and miserable as life is, many are afraid of risking the little they do have and try to make the most out of the bad choices they made early. One twenty-six-year-old man with ten years of schooling unloads and washes hogs in a meat-packing business. The job is steady, but he is dissatisfied with "the whole set-up." The smell nauseates him so he cannot even eat lunch. But he has just bought a ramshackle bungalow and cannot afford the risk of changing to another, possibly less secure job.

This situation typifies Stage 2, young persons entering the job market early with little qualifications for work. They take the first job offered to them, usually found through chance and without any consideration of its potential. Very often these turn into blind alleys. The parents, happy to see a little extra money coming in, do not give any guidance that could help their children avoid this costly early mistake.

So the young person takes the dead-end jobs, gets married, and as the family begins to grow, the family cycle squeeze begins—Stage 3. Housing is more expensive and more difficult to find for a larger family, the mother is less able to work, and as the years pass, the couple finds its hopes fading as the immediate needs build up. In this position the poor often engage in what is called "compensatory consumption." They have given up on the long-range plans they once nurtured, so they try to ease the pain by buying other things. Like all of us, the poor have been trained by society to want, but the poor are not good shoppers. They are generally uninformed about sales, comparative shopping, evaluation of advice by salespersons. They are susceptible to the "easy credit" offered by exploiting merchants, particularly since they are not eligible for the credit under more conventional provisions. As a result the poor pay more for inferior quality than anyone else.

Ultimately, purchases stop altogether, though the needs continue to mount. The squeeze often gets so tight that one parent leaves and the family begins to break down—Stage 4.

Of the 5 million poor families in the United States, more than half are run by a woman with no husband present. This account might show the beginning of the breakdown. "All this needing and wanting is about to drive me crazy. Now I've got double trouble. My husband is a good man, but every time they fire him or lay him off, he takes it out on me and the kids. He gets his little bottle and starts nipping it. By the time he nips to the bottom, he's mad with the whole world. Then the kids and I get it, especially Norman Jr. Those two don't get along at all. That boy keeps telling him he'll kill him if he keeps beating up on me. I wouldn't be surprised someday if he'll just up and do it."

At an early age many poor children experience this kind of strife; they see their fathers or mothers leave to live with other partners, or see other men come to live with their own mothers and sisters.

Still, the nature of poverty makes its victims pragmatic. "If a man has anything and offers to help you out," one woman explains, "you don't say to him, 'But you'll have to marry me first.' You take what he offers right off, and offer what you have in return. Of course, you hope that someday he will want to make it legal. But beggars can't be choosers."

These are the stages of life, then, through which millions of our fellow citizens must move. The poor seem to know personally what the sociologists conclude statistically about the causes and effects of poverty. They even know the ways out, but the tragedy is that they cannot do what has to be done. One woman seems to sum it up: "When there are children, you usually have to watch out, because if you don't you'll have too many. And without education, and luck, you can't support your children. So that's why you should try to show your children that going to school and finishing school is for their good. Not so that you can hold your head and brag and say 'that's my child'. . . . But because this world is getting weaker and wiser and it's going to take two parents to try and show a child the facts of life and the facts of marriage."

Many look to education as the hope of the future but the schools often seem inadequate to handle the great challenge. As one commentator put it, "In the school it's the same as in the home—a woman with too many kids." One such school in eastern Kentucky can be reached only by crossing a muddy creek from an unpaved road that winds its way into one of many blind valleys where the coal miners—many of them unemployed—live. The teacher is in charge of five grades—fourth, fifth, sixth, seventh, and eighth—in her half of the wooden building that comprises the school. In the adjacent room a younger woman teaches grades one, two, and three. Bare bulbs provide light, and a pot-bellied stove affords heat in winter. Most of the thirty-eight children in the room work on their own, the older ones helping the younger, the faster giving aid to the slow. One child has no shoes, many have no socks, and several look prematurely old."

Though physical conditions and numbers may vary from place to place, one constant in most classrooms for the poor is the high porportion of failure, of dropouts, of reading and learning disabilities. Educators point to the deficiencies with which the poor children come to school, their lack of familiarity with books, pencils, crayons, pictures, and they concede that for many the school is unable to overcome the damaging effects of their lives at home and on the streets. Despite the billions of dollars poured into the schools in recent years, school systems are still turning out many children who cannot read or do arithmetic.

At the same time, employers are demanding greater skills of the people they hire. Unskilled labor is being replaced by machinery in so many areas. Cities are becoming white-collar factories for which education is critical. Those who are illiterate are in trouble. Even lower level jobs—once held by the poor—are now being held by people with more qualifications who cannot find work at their own level. Employers who must pay a minimum wage of $2.90 an hour are looking for the most qualified people they can get. In many small businesses positions that would at one time be filled by the poor now are eliminated because of the high minimum wage.

During a recent widespread sag in the economy, with a resulting increase in unemployment, the National Federation of Settlements and Neighborhoods Centers collected these reports from its agencies. *From Detroit:* Junior club members have been unable to pay the fifty cents annual membership fee. At Christmas children mentioned that they did not expect to receive any toys or new clothes. Adults sit home and look helpless, depressed, not interested in participating in neighborhood life. Drunkenness increases. *From Chicago:* We see worried men and women, neglected health needs, evictions, desertion, creditors repossessing furniture, inadequate diets. *From Cleveland:* Garnishments, overbuying on credit, increased dependency, crime.

Crime and joblessness seem to go hand-in-hand with the poor, especially among the young. Studies predict that 48 percent of the hard-core unemployed can be expected at one time or another to commit crime. "The streets make you do crazy things," one man said, "when there ain't nothing wrong with you and you can't get a job."

A vicious circle spins as the poor without employment drift into crime, making future employment more difficult. The middle class abandons the crime area, taking away business that had provided some employment and, in the process, taking away the community's tax base. Schools and other services decline, and the poor sink deeper into poverty.

The problem of the poor is massive and complex, baffling the efforts of the government and many private organizations. For job programs alone, the federal government has spent more than $40 billion over the last ten years, yet there are more eighteen- to twenty-four-year-olds in local jails than in these programs.

Still, we must not stop hoping and trying. We cannot stop if only because of the divine command to continue: "The poor will never cease out of the land: therefore I command you: you shall open wide your hand to your brother, to the needy and to the poor in the land" (Deut. 15:11).

Many local groups throughout the country have been funded by the government and by the Campaign for Human Development to create programs of various types to help the poor. One helped a Legal Aid project take on the U.S. Agriculture Department to implement a congressionally-mandated provision of the Food Stamp program. Another helped a coalition of textile workers win disability rights for victims of job-related lung ailments. Many others have helped the poor in the areas of education, housing, transportation, health, and just about every phase of life.

A small parish group can seek the aid of the CHD or government agencies in initiating preschool programs, health and homemaker services, recreational activities, job training and counseling assistance. In many areas these programs are already in existence but need workers to aid the professionals in reaching the people who most need the help. Providing the workers, finding the "lost" victims, and joining the two, could in itself be a worthy group endeavor.

Just informing other Christians of the plight of the poor would do much toward the improvement of their condition. Set up reservoirs of information, provide speakers to groups in the community explaining the severity of the problem. Checking out the treatment given to the poor in local and parish schools can help the poor directly, as well as indirectly, by teaching all youth to be more aware of the less fortunate.

In this regard, parents can teach their own children to be more sensitive to our wasteful use of resources, and the best way to teach this is through example. We can live the admonition of St. Augustine who said, "He who has a surplus possesses the goods of another." We can simplify our living and contribute the resulting savings to those who need it. We can sell the big gas-guzzler and buy a more economical car, with the poor being the beneficiary of our austerity. We can do the same with money saved by making our own clothes, cutting down on luxuries, delicacies, trips. To involve the whole family in these decisions would go a long way toward spreading Christ's attitude toward the poor.

We might take the example of Marilyn H—— who bought a new coat on sale, and gave the old, usable coat to someone else. While on vacation, Marilyn sublet her apartment to a single parent for half the rent; another woman will use Marilyn's car while she is away.

With the right attitude we can use our creativity to find many ways we can, as individuals and as a community, to help the poor. In doing so we can come closer to Christ: "The spirit of the Lord is upon me, because he has anointed me to preach the good news to the poor. He has sent me to proclaim release to the captives and recovery of sight to the blind, to set at liberty those who are oppressed, to proclaim the acceptable year of the Lord" (Luke 4:18–19).

COSMO F. FERRARA, Ed.D. Dr. Ferrara is a former teacher. He is currently writing on subjects related to education and family living.

Facts on Poor Families

FAMILIES AND TOTAL INCOME

Total Yearly Income	Millions of Families	Percent
$25,000 or more	12.8	22.4%
$15,000 to 25,000	18.1	31.7%
$10,000 to 15,000	10.6	18.4%
$5,000 to 10,000	10.4	18.1%
$5,000 or below	5.3	9.3%

FAMILY RELATIONSHIPS

Total number of poor families	5,311,000
Families with husband and wife	2,524,000
Families with male head, no wife	177,000
Families with female head, no husband	2,610,000

NUMBER OF CHILDREN AND POVERTY

Percentage of families that are poor having	Number of children under 18
12%	0,1,2
17%	3
23%	4
36%	5
49%	6

RACE AND POVERTY

Number of Poor (Individuals)	% of all poor	% of total pop.
7,726,000 Blacks	29%	12%
2,700,000 Hispanics	10%	6%
16,416,000 Whites	61%	72%

FAMILY TO FAMILY

Catherine Zandler

"The family of God lives next door and may be in need." To love God and to love one's neighbor are the two basic commandments of the New Testament—tenets reiterated throughout the Gospel message. In Matthew, we clearly learn that we will be judged on our response to the needs of the hungry, the homeless, the oppressed. In John, we are told that "the poor we will have always with us." The statement is not just a prophecy but more likely an indictment that we have failed to solve the problems of equal sharing of the world's God-given resources with all of God's people.

In his Apostolic Exhortation, *On Evangelization in the Modern World*, Paul VI points out that "between evangelization and human advancement-development and liberation—there are profound links. These include links of an anthropological order, because the man who is to be evangelized is not an abstract being but is subject to social and economic questions."

During the past few months, John Paul II has laid it on the line. At Puebla, Mexico, he noted: "Particular care must be given to forming a social conscience at all levels and in all sectors. When injustices worsen and the distance between rich and poor increases distressingly, the social doctrine, in a form which is creative and open to the broad fields of the Church's presence, must be a valuable instrument for formation and action. This holds good particularly for the laity."

Then a few short weeks later, in his first encyclical, *The Redeemer of Man*, our Pope calls for the whole of the Church, as the society and community of the people of God on earth, to serve all mankind. "We must likewise understand how each one of us must share in this mission and service," he notes.

The path is clearly defined. However, the signposts may not be as legible. For we may ask, how do I find my neighbor who is in need? Perhaps he is a neighbor only in the sense of the broader community. But is the command to serve any less valid? It seems, as the People of God, we cannot justify living in a vacuum, one in which our daily paths shun those families in need of the basic necessities of life itself, in need of emotional support and in need of the spiritual refreshment of seeing Christ in each of us.

The challenge is to identify the methods by which we can serve our neighbor in a more personal way than that of giving our spare dollars to impersonal worthy causes, in a way that brings us face to face with the hidden poor, in a way that reaches out and enables us to touch the least of our brethren. There is no single path to this service, but we present here three simple, concrete models that are working to bring us into contact with our neighbor in need.

BUILDING CHURCH WITHIN AND WITHOUT

On the first Sunday in Lent, St. Jerome's Parish in Phoenix, Arizona, undertook a positive Lenten sacrificial project. Following an appropriate homily, a basket of suggestions was passed through the congregation. Each member—adult, teen-agers, and children—was asked to draw a slip (white for adults, yellow for teens, and blue for children). A sampling of ideas included:

For Adults:
Fix a meal for someone who is ill.
Invite a lonely person to dinner.
Help someone with a home repair job.

For Teens:
Provide transportation for someone who is in need of it.
Be especially kind to someone you don't really like.
Do a kind deed for your parents—without being asked.

For Children:
Offer to help an elderly person with something.
Keep your room clean and picked-up for one week.
Help an unpopular classmate with something.

Each member who completed his or her task was asked to add a stick-on brick to the plywood church placed on the left side of the altar. Parishioners were invited to undertake the project as a family or to come up with their own ideas of how to build a "spiritual house" while the actual construction of a church was underway.

The acts of kindness, charity, and justice become the bricks and mortar of the community of St. Jerome's. And it is indeed a family-to-family project. In the case of one family, the father helped a needy family repair its sewer. Supper was delayed for all family members as he provided the expertise and labor to help out a neighbor in need. The teen-age son mowed the lawn for the blind lady who lived across the street. Now it's an every-other-week occasion. And the young daughter learned how to make her own bed. Community was built both within the family of parents and children, and within the parish family.

The three-fold mission of service need not be limited to Lent nor to a parish involved in physically erecting a church. Perhaps, more real than symbolic is the need of the parish whose physical plant is complete but whose real challenge is to build a community. The path to understanding, compassion, and sharing one's life with another is limited only by the imagination and innovativeness of the Family of God.

ADOPTING A NEEDY FAMILY

Our second model is a classroom project of "adopting a needy family" by eighth grade students in a parochial school or religious education class.

Obvious projects, such as providing food for a Thanksgiving dinner or a Christmas party with presents for all members of the family, are standard. One class, however, fulfilled the "adopted" family's need for a refrigerator and stove, and found a new job and home for "their family." The family had lived and worked as tenants on a small farm for years. With the advent of a new owner whose goal was a housing development, both the job and the home were gone. Short of a distressing personal experience, no better lesson in economic justice could have been gained.

The year was climaxed with a party given by the family in their new home for all the students in the class.

It is much more than a classroom project. Since eighth grade students cannot drive, parents become involved in visits to the family and in projects to meet specific needs of the family. The role of room mother for the class became a much sought-after plum. The year's activities, which also included helping at a children's day care center in the inner city and visits to nursing homes and senior citizen centers, heightened the awareness of adults as well as children. It was a far cry from the traditional ice-cream and cake Valentine parties of most room mothers. (A slide presentation detailing the experiences of a full academic year is available for loan from the Diocese of Phoenix Human Development Council.)

Keys to the success of this family participation and awareness model are:

1) Careful selection of the family, perhaps recommended by the diocese's social service agency.
2) The family assisted gives more than it gains and it must understand the project and be willing to openly share the causes and effects of its poverty in a nonemotional manner.
3) The visits, except for very special occasions, should include only four or five students at a time.
4) Each visit is followed by a feedback session, conducted by a teacher or moderator who is sensitive to the learning process occurring as students share the insights they gained and who will detail the needs of the family so that the class as a whole can undertake to resolve them.
5) Parents must be involved throughout and be willing but not dominating participants in the project.

PARISH VOLUNTEER SERVICES

The final model is a neighborhood volunteer service project. Patterned after the National Conference of Catholic Charities Parish Outreach Project, this program offers an ongoing structured process for offering opportunities for families to serve other families, to help and to be helped within a parish community without regard to religious affiliation.

Few parish communities, if any, do not have people within their boundaries whose needs are not served by existing public and private agencies. The first step is determining some of those needs; the second is a full parish effort, centering around a homily at mass, to recruit volunteers to set up a small volunteer office where phone calls can be taken for such services as visiting a sick or homebound person, providing transportation to medical appointments, necessary shopping and church services on Sunday, sitting with a handicapped child or elderly relative so that parents can go about needed errands or even just have time off together, bringing meals to an ill person, or performing simple household chores, such as lawnmowing or shoveling snow.

Both adults and teen-agers can participate in all of these activities, which include office staffers and service volunteers. Although an ongoing one-to-one relationship between one family and another is not structured into this program—for who can determine which personalities mesh into friendships?—such relationships do happen. The prime beneficiaries are not necessarily the family receiving help, but frequently are those giving help. Empathy not sympathy, rapport not reproach, is the result.

Who gains the most is difficult to say. The volunteer gains understanding and knowledge on a firsthand experiential basis. Volunteers find that those states without an Aid to Dependent Children–Unemployed Parent Program force fathers to desert their families so that the family can qualify for public assistance; they know that the stipend, even supplemented by Food Stamps, leaves a less than adequate income to provide basic needs; they recognize that poor health (and serious illness) is one of the major causes of economic dependency; they discover that lack of education and training equates with submarginal, temporary employment that carries none of the benefits the average American expects: unemployment insurance, workmen's compensation, health insurance, retirement plans. They do not have to be sociologists or economists to recognize that the lack of job opportunities is more relevant than laziness or unwillingness to work for most of those who live a marginal existence.

Thus the basis for advocacy by the average Catholic family for those far less fortunate is formed. Support for such programs as better income assistance, comprehensive health care, full employment (jobs for all able-bodied adults), safe, sanitary housing, and low-cost transportation reaches beyond those needs that can be alleviated because one family cares enough to share.

Given the limited resources of the world, the middle and upper income family can only learn from the life-style of the less fortunate. Coping with poverty is a real strength of the poor, one that can teach most of us a great deal on how to conserve the world's resources. Those living a simplified life-style by choice are sure to learn from those living simply without choice.

As for the less fortunate family, these projects offer *hope*—a necessary ingredient to achieving a better life on earth and beyond. Not only does the alleviation of immediate problems help them, the assistance voluntarily, lovingly, and understandingly given by another family sustains self-respect and self-image—an ingredient sadly lacking in most governmental assistance programs. Given the opportunity to gain and hold a job, to encourage children in the pursuit of education, to live in decent, safe surroundings, the disadvantaged family of today, experienced in withstanding hardships, may well be the truly self-sufficient family of tomorrow.

Faith, hope, and charity can spring eternal when one family helps another!

CATHERINE ZANDLER. Mrs. Zandler holds a B.A. in Journalism from Wichita State University and is Program and Resource Director for the Human Development Council of the Diocese of Phoenix. She is a member of the National Committee of the U.S.C.C. Campaign for Human Development.

THE HANDICAPPED

Sister Sheila Haskett, O.S.F.

Strange. There's always such a sameness. Same setting—hospital, sterilized, impersonal smells and sounds. Same cast of characters: the doctor in a terrible hurry, the nurses exchanging significant glances, the mother vaguely apprehensive, the father knotted up in disbelief, questioning *What? How? Why?* The baby is placidly sleeping. Same script—almost no script actually. The doctor, if he says anything, says something like, "It's defective," or "You've got a mongoloid here." Period. Exit. End of the opening scene in the life of the handicapped child. Meanwhile, the bottom has just fallen out of his parents' lives.

No parent expects his child to be in any way inferior to himself or to his peers. When it happens, he or she is usually totally unprepared. The terms used, "Down's Syndrome," "minimal brain dysfunction," etc., mean nothing. In reminiscing on those very difficult early days, parents will often say, "If I just knew then what I know now, how different everything would have been!" and almost invariably they add, "My friends didn't understand. The Church didn't help and I began to wonder what God was punishing me for." It is indeed tragic that the parents of a newborn handicapped child feel alone, unworthy, abandoned.

But then, no one expects the children of his friends, neighbors, or fellow parishioners to make up the statistics of the handicapped population, either. When it happens, though, what can one *do*?

First, it must be remembered that parenting any child in today's very complex world is not an easy task. Parenting a handicapped child is considerably more difficult. When the diagnosis is rendered, it almost invariably comes as a complete surprise and a stunning blow to the parent who could not possibly have prepared for this situation. Compounding the agony is the effect of this birth on the parents' marital stability, on their relationship with grandparents and other relatives, on their other children, and on their social lives. Their world (or at least the relationships in it) has literally crashed around them!

Typically, there are certain fairly well-defined stages that parents go through in adjustment and ultimately acceptance. The first stage is that of disbelief—"This can't really be happening to me, it'll all go away by tomorrow"; denial—"There's nothing really wrong—lots of kids start out a little slow"; grieving—"I mourn for the child who might have been." The greatest service that can be rendered at this time is the showing of compassion, a listening ear, as the parent expresses his or her pain and bewilderment. *Don't agree with their misstatements; don't make evaluative statements.* "I am here. I care" is all that should be conveyed by word and by small, but consistently paid attentions.

The second stage is characterized by fear—"What will people think of me?"; frustration—"Nothing can change, my child is a human vegetable!"; bitterness—"What have I done to deserve this?" Reassurance is most needed at this point. A handicapped child can be reasonably explained, *but need not be apologized for.* Rich and poor, famous and obscure, very good and not so very good people have had developmentally disabled children: Charles de Gaulle, Beverly Sills, Rose Kennedy, Dale Evans. *The situation is not without hope. The vast majority of developmentally disabled children, if given proper care, stimulation, education, and training can grow up to be productive, happy adults.* Some of them even become famous in their own right as Yoshihiko Yamamoto, for example, a developmentally disabled man whose artistic creations have earned him recognition as one of the outstanding artists of Japan.

A visit to a program where handicapped children are functioning well might help the parent to visualize what might be expected for the child. A visit with a parent who has gone through the experience of having a developmentally disabled child and coped well, or viewing the film "Mother Tiger, Mother Tiger" might also help. Several books have been written by parents describing their reaction to their child. These might also reassure the distraught parent that the situation can be a positive value in their lives.

A mother, Angela M. Schreiber, recently wrote:

> In five short years, Yvonne has given us more than we can ever give her. Little things are more important; working together with the child we love so much has brought us closer and deepened our love for one another. How far her mental development goes seems less and less important, perhaps because her love for us is so pure, unquestioning and gentle.
>
> Each morning, she awakes with childish delight to greet the day. Yes, she loves God's creations—the sunshine, the rain, the flowers. Our beautiful little Yvonne is very much a part of it all. I just needed time to understand that God gave us His special blessing.

Another mother, Phoebe Ballard, commented:

> It has been slow in coming, but at last I believe Tod and I understand what that first woman in that first school in Los Angeles said: *Are you an Einstein? Do you feel frustrated?*
>
> We realize now that Wayne is an individual, with just as much to give to his society as any other individual, that the joy, the beauty, the love he gives are not less than what poets, painters, and writers give. We need no longer feel stricken that our son is a mongoloid, but may instead be proud of him for what he produces.

During one of these two stages it might be very helpful to put the parent in touch with the local Association for Retarded Citizens and their Parent Helper Program. These are people who have walked this road themselves and are eager to share what they have learned to spare others the pain they have experienced. They are listed in the telephone book, and usually have a state office in the capitol city.

The third stage is characterized by inquiry and search for an accurate, differential diagnosis, treatment plans, training programs, medical and educational resources. Parents are rarely able to accept the first diagnosis, and it is often a form of catharsis for them to take their child from doctor to doctor, clinic to clinic, specialist to specialist. Eventually, physically and financially exhausted, they are ready to hear the truth. At this point help can take the form of sharing information on how to feed and care for the child, resources for respites so that marriage, social, and other family responsibilities can be carried on.

Not all parents go through all stages, or go through the stages in quite the same sequence. For some people it takes many, many years to accept on the inside as well as in outward appearances.

One of the most painful aspects of being the parent of a developmentally disabled child is the attitude too frequently displayed by members of the helping professions. Rejection of their child is often felt as rejection of themselves. The humiliation of being treated in a patronizing manner—"Oh, you poor thing! Let *me* help you. *I* have the answers!"—can, over a period of time, harden into embittering resentment.

A person with a problem needs to be met with understanding for himself as a person and with help for the problem; it is not helpful to be considered a problem person. A woman who had worked for many years with special children and their families tells how this very important distinction became clear to her. She had gone to see the family physician who gently broke the very painful news that she had diabetes. "It was a terrible blow," she said, "but I *could* handle it. I was managing the diagnosis pretty well until an attending nurse came in and referred to me as a diabetic. Suddenly I was completely devastated. I could bear the thought of *having* something undesirable, but I could not bear *being* something undesirable."

The language used in referring to a child and his handicapping condition can be very wounding. It can also be very healing if it expresses affection and respect, sympathy but never pity. It is a realistic and humbling admission that, given the same problem to deal with, one would probably not cope even as well as the parents of the handicapped child.

Finally, in becoming deeply involved with the problem of the handicapped person, there is a very real danger that we may come to perceive *them* as problems rather than as people who happen to have a problem. To do this is to lose the beauty, the mystery of their lives, these lives through which God works to clearly show forth his ways with man (John 9:3).

Jean Vanier, founder of the L'Arche communities scattered about the world, once commented:

> . . . Because the mentally handicapped lack a strong rational self, they do not have a consciousness of power. They develop a capacity for *friendship*, rather than for *efficiency*. Their capacity for love is more immediate and more developed than that of other men. They have shown me what it is to live simply, to love tenderly, to receive openly, to be humble in weakness, to be confident in difficulties and to accept handicaps and hardships with love. And in a mysterious way in their lives they have revealed Jesus to everyone of us.

It is important to understand that developmentally disabled persons have a tremendous need to *give* their gifts as well as receive the ones that are offered them. They need to have their gifts accepted with respect. If a teacher or a parent wants always to give, and never stops to listen, never stops to receive, there can be no real communion with the handicapped person. Love requires a communion. It must be a receiving as well as a giving. One must become aware of the wonderful gifts that these special individuals have to give—the wonderful gift of recognizing the innate goodness and value of other persons, for example. One must recognize and humbly *receive* these gifts before one can claim to truly love this handicapped individual. The greatest gift one can give a developmentally disabled person is to give him the opportunity to *give.* One must be able to say "thank you" before one can truly say "I love you."

SISTER SHEILA HASKETT, O.S.F., Ph.D. Sister Sheila holds a doctorate in Counseling and Behavioral Studies from the University of Wisconsin. She is the Administrator of St. Coletta's School in Jefferson, Wisconsin and is the President of the National Apostolate with Mentally Retarded Persons.

HEALING WITH THE RETARDED

Brigid O'Donnell

"Joan, did you hear about the group home that's supposed to move into the old Stanford house? Just who do they think they are?! I don't want a bunch of retarded men around *my* children! Who knows what they'll do?"

"I agree, Liz. This is a respectable neighborhood. Besides that, Pete and I have put a lot of work into our house. We didn't sink time and money into it to have its value decreased by that group of crazy people. They should be in an institution where they won't get hurt and where they can't harm anyone."

"Well, I'm not going to stand for it. Jim and I are starting a petition to keep them out of this neighborhood. Do you and Pete want to sign it?"

"I'm sure we will. Give me a call later, O.K.? I've got to get supper on."

When Liz went to bed that night the group home was still on her mind. She was concerned about her children and the home she had worked so hard to improve. Her husband was pretty much in agreement with her strong feelings but suggested they look into more facts before they do anything rash.

Liz and Joan's comments and reactions to a group home are not atypical. They are fearful of the unknown and have bought into the stereotypes of retarded people that society projects and even condones. Jim has the same gut feeling but wants to ground it in reality. Most likely none of them have met a retarded person or know someone who has a retarded child. And until they do or until they research some of the facts, their attitudes will probably remain closed and judgmental.

In Jim and Liz's parish there are several families who have a retarded child. They don't know any of them, partly because there are few opportunities for their retarded youngsters to feel part of the Church, partly because some of the retarded children and adults blend into the congregation and are not visible. In their parish of 1500 families, forty-five are affected by some degree of mental retardation.

If Jim and Liz were to talk with any of these families, they might have a different attitude and understanding about mentally retarded people, their parents and siblings. Given the opportunity, this is what parents might say.

Mrs. Armstrong

"I'm Madeleine Armstrong and I have four children. My second oldest, Kevin, is mildly retarded. He's thirteen—at that terrible transition age—and is in a special class at school. He reads at about a fourth grade level but has more difficulty with math. He's in with the other junior high kids for gym, art, and music—mainstreaming they call it—and does O.K. His real talent is in woodworking; he made me some beautiful bookends. He likes sports but is never chosen for the team; he won a gold medal, however, in the Special Olympics last year for the hundred-meter dash. He's so proud of that medal!

"It's hard for Kevin because he's not readily accepted by the rest of the kids his age. He doesn't have any physical handicap; he just finds schoolwork difficult. Because he's in a special room at the junior high, the kids call him 'dummy' and other names. You wouldn't believe how many times he comes home in tears. What can I say to him?

"Kevin just doesn't know how to fit in, and I don't know what to tell him. He has a lot of the same interests as other boys his age, but he still enjoys doing things with the younger boys. Luckily Dan and Joe, his brothers aged ten and twelve, often take Kevin with them when they do things. But no one bothers to call Kevin and ask him to come along; I don't like doing the asking all the time, and I don't think Dan and Joe should always have to take that responsibility. Susie, sixteen, is at the age when *any* little brother can be a pain, but especially Kevin. She doesn't want to bring her friends home because Kevin can be a pest or will say or do inappropriate things. I have to respect her as well as look out for my son. She sometimes resents hav-

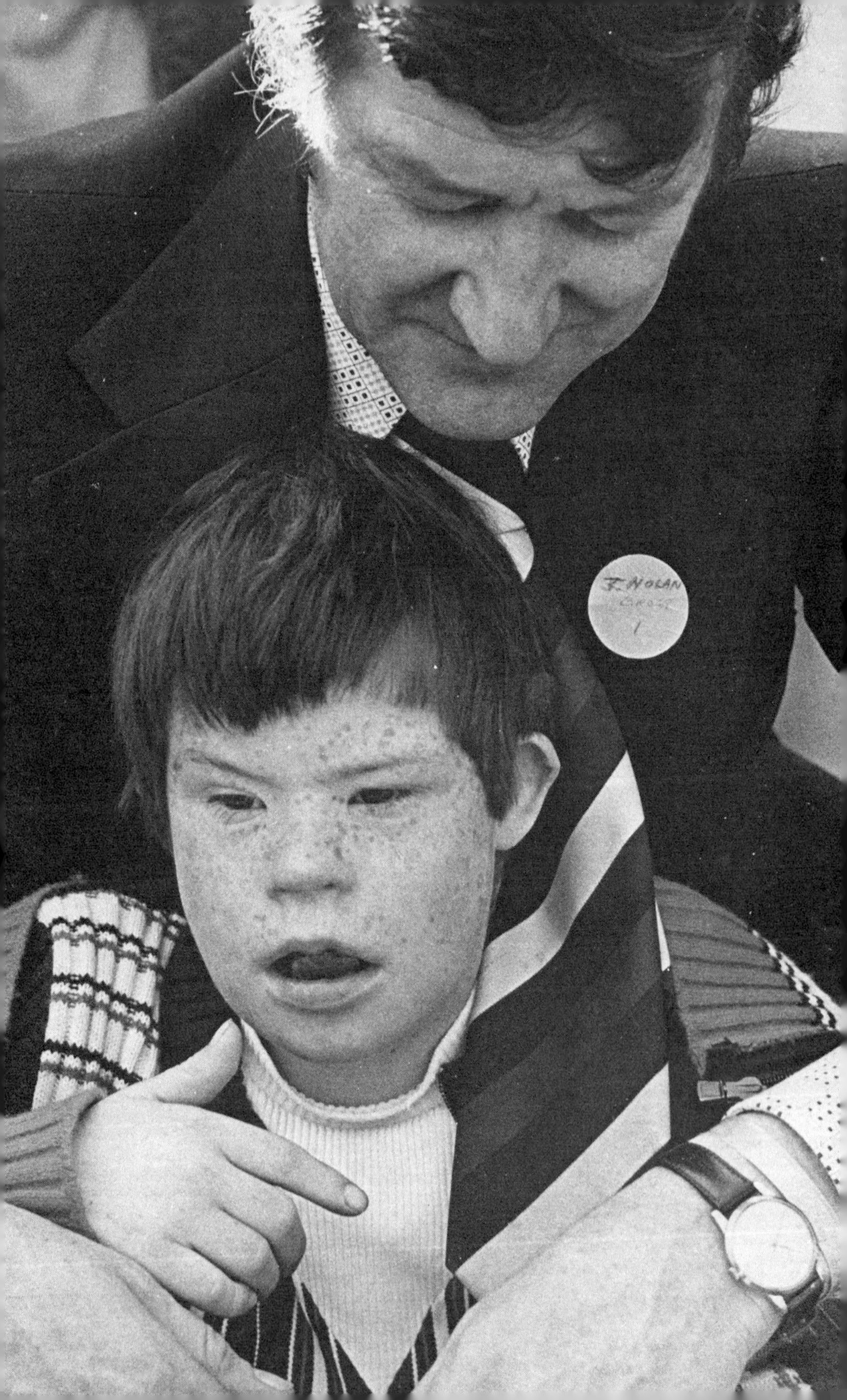
F. NOLAN

ing to babysit, but Kevin isn't quite able to handle the responsibility of being alone or with his two younger brothers.

"My husband left because he couldn't cope with the pressures of having a handicapped child. He wasn't able to see the good aspects of Kevin or his impact on the family. It took me a long time to deal with the fact that Kevin is retarded and needs special help in school and at home. Some days I run out of patience, but other days are a joy. I look back at when Kevin was a toddler and when he started school, and I made it through those years. I have different problems to face in the near future, like his learning to drive and dating, finding a job. I also worry about what will happen to Kevin when I die. While he can do many things on his own I think he'll always need someone to help him. I don't want to place that responsibility on Susie or Joe or Dan unless they want it. I hope there will be a group home where he can live and that will help him to continue to grow and learn.

"One of the hardest things for me is people who don't want to take the time to understand Kevin. Because he doesn't look different than other kids his age but sometimes acts inappropriately, people sometimes make ugly comments or walk away in disgust. Instead of taking Kevin for who he is, they compare him to some set of standards; when he doesn't measure up, they criticize him or me as a parent. If they have questions I wish they'd ask; I'd be happy to try to answer them.

"The parish does provide a religious education class for Kevin and others who need special help, and I'm very grateful for that. But Kevin needs to be with other teenagers, too. I wish the Youth Group would invite him when they go roller-skating or do other social things. Maybe Kevin could help in some parish activities, like setting tables for a luncheon or washing dishes, stuffing bulletins, or helping with babysitting on Sunday. I know I could call and ask if Kevin could be included in these things, but I'd like him to be invited by someone from the parish. Then I'd know he's really wanted and isn't being pitied.

"This sounds like a lot of complaining, and I don't want anyone to think that life is only a problem for me or my family. I could spend as much time telling you about the great times we have together or the joy when Kevin succeeds at something. But maybe if people understand some of the additional worries in a family with a mildly retarded child they'd be more patient toward me and my needs and requests."

Mr. Simpson

"I'm Ralph Simpson and I'm sixty-five. I have three children: Angela, forty; Robert, thirty-seven; and Terry, twenty-six. My wife died last year, so now it's just Terry and me. Terry works at the sheltered workshop making candles. She helps clean the house and does some of the cooking, too. It's hard for her to read the recipes, but once she knows how to make something she doesn't forget! Terry loves the grandchildren—has a knack for playing with them. She's great to have around; I don't know what I would do without her.

"Marie and I didn't always think that way. When Terry was born with Down's Syndrome, the doctor and several friends told us to put her away in an institution. 'You're too old to deal with raising another youngster, much less one who won't even be able to do anything,' they told us. They really made us think. After all, we weren't young, and we didn't know if we could do the right things for Terry. Luckily we had a few people who encouraged us to try to keep Terry at home, and they promised to help us. A couple from the Association for Retarded Citizens came to see us and offered to help. It was good to know there were other parents feeling the same way we did—guilty at having brought a handicapped child into the world, angry with God for 'punishing' us, lost in medical jargon, bewildered by additional expenses, wondering how Angela and Robert would accept Terry, frightened about the future for all of us.

"The Church wasn't much help twenty years ago. We tried to teach Terry her prayers, to love other people, something about Jesus. But we needed some help. The priest told us that Terry was a saint and would go straight to heaven;

she didn't need religion classes like other kids. Marie and I *knew* that Terry wasn't a saint, but we couldn't convince anyone at church! So we took Terry to church with us on Sunday, but that was it for religion.

"We tried again when the new pastor came, but he said the parish debt was too high and there weren't enough kids for a special class, and besides that there weren't any teachers. So we went to the head of the Education Committee and asked them to please provide something for our daughter. After three years (and finding four other families who wanted special education classes) the parish began a program. It was small but it was—and is—the joy of Terry's life. It makes her feel like she really belongs to the Church. I just wish people would have been more willing to listen to what we needed to help our daughter grow spiritually.

"My biggest concern now is what's going to happen to Terry. I'm in good health now, but I won't be around forever. Angela and Robert love Terry, but they have families of their own. I've got her name in for a group home, but there's a long waiting list. That's a big worry for me."

Mr. and Mrs. Jennings

"We're Kathy and Mike Jennings. We have five children—Donna, age twelve; Matt, age eleven; Bill, age eight; Johnny, age six; and Laurie, three. Our fourth child, Johnny, is severely retarded. He can't walk or feed himself, and he isn't toilet-trained. He has no speech, but he has a beautiful smile that he flashes when he sees someone he recognizes.

"We recently made the decision to place Johnny in a residential facility for mentally retarded persons. It was a very difficult decision, but we feel we made it for the best interests of Johnny, ourselves, and the rest of our children. It was not done without many tears and much guilt about not being able to parent adequately. On top of feeling guilty about giving birth to a severely retarded child, now we have to deal with what appears to others to be rejection. Believe us, we're not rejecting Johnny at all.

"While all of us love Johnny very deeply, we also are realistic about the amount of time it takes to physically care for Johnny. Feeding, clothing, bathing, and diapering a baby is one thing; giving the same care to a six-year-old who weighs thirty-five pounds is quite another! Not only is it physically draining, but it's emotionally exhausting as well. There just wasn't enough energy to give to Johnny and the other children, too.

"The children rarely complained and always pitched in to help us, and we tried to continue to do the things we liked to do together, like camping, but it got harder and harder to do them. We love all our children and can't have life revolve around just one individual's needs.

"Another consideration was schooling for Johnny. Even though PL 94–142 assures free and appropriate education for all handicapped persons aged three to twenty-one, not all school districts can meet the specialized needs of someone like our Johnny. Now that he's at the residential facility he's learning to use a simple word board to communicate. Our school district couldn't have provided that kind of instruction.

"One of our greatest fears was to have another child after Johnny. We just didn't want to take that risk! When we discovered that we were expecting our fifth child all sorts of things crossed our minds. We prayed for the courage to accept whatever God would send us. Those nine months weren't easy; nothing could calm our frightened anticipation. When Laurie was born we rejoiced that all appeared to be well. Perhaps the more difficult thing was seeing our baby able to do things that Johnny would never master.

"What we would have appreciated from the Church was some help in making the decision to institutionalize Johnny or support as we struggled with our daily routine. Babysitting service during Mass is great if your child can come to the church, but that was a major project for us. We wonder if anyone ever thought of offering to sit at home? We should have made the request ourselves, but we didn't know whom to ask and even felt we shouldn't request something extraordinary.

"We did belong to a discussion club and the other couples who came knew about our situation, but they seemed uneasy and reluctant to talk when we brought up our son. We didn't want pity; we just wanted others to learn about people like Johnny, and sometimes we needed an ear to help us see if we were on the right moral track."

Mr. and Mrs. Baker

"Our names are Sarah and Dennis Baker. We have two daughters, Roseanne and Karen. We're in our early fifties; Roseanne is married and has a son; Karen is twenty and just graduating from special classes at the high school. Karen is an attractive young woman who adores children. She reads fairly well, and because her handwriting isn't very good, she's learned to type. She'll be starting a job as a file clerk in an insurance company in a few weeks. Right now she's on vacation with three of her friends and their teacher from high school. She's worked hard to save the money for this trip.

"We have some of the same concerns as Mrs. Armstrong about the future, but our immediate problem is dealing with Karen's desire to move away from home and be married like her sister. Karen is mildly retarded, so she has some difficulty in managing a household completely on her own, but she could do it with minimum supervision. A group home would be too structured for Karen; she's more capable than that, but she isn't able to live alone. If only there were someone with whom she could share an apartment, or if she could live alone and have someone check in on her occasionally. Like any other person her age, she wants to move away from home. We agree, but the possibilities are so limited!

"Our other worry is Karen and her boyfriend Steve. They'd like to be married, but we just don't think either of them is capable of dealing with the responsibilities and pressures of marriage. We can't convince them that marriage takes more than falling in love and hoping that everything will turn out right. We've talked with Karen about sex, but we're concerned about all the time she spends with Steve. It's difficult to know what to say or not to say about contraceptives to your attractive, young, mildly retarded daughter. While she may be able someday to be married, perhaps to Steve, they probably couldn't take on the responsibility of a child in addition to their own relationship. We need guidance from the priests and from other parishioners to help us look at all the aspects of Karen's life and our responsibilities to her."

Perhaps if Jim and Liz met Mrs. Armstrong, Mr. Simpson, the Jennings, the Bakers, or any other family with a mentally handicapped child, they wouldn't be so quick to condemn the group home in their neighborhood. Or they might see if their parish is offering special religious instruction or has wheelchair accessible buildings. They might examine their own attitudes of openness toward other parents' difficulties or look at the attitudes their children have toward mentally handicapped individuals. They might not stereotype mentally handicapped persons as being dangerous or stupid. They might even see the beauty and joy that a mentally handicapped person can bring to a family and to a community. Most importantly they might realize that each of us is handicapped in some way and each of us has unique gifts to offer to our families, our church, and our community.

About 6 million persons in the United States share this condition, but they aren't the only ones who are affected. Add at least one parent for each (about 9 million) and at least one sibling (another 9 million). And that's without mentioning other family members, friends, or neighbors. A minimum of 24 million people are touched in some way by mental retardation. While another statistic (3 percent of the population) might make us think the problem is small, 24 million people know that it's one of the major issues in their lives.

The American Association on Mental Deficiency defines mental retardation as "subaverage intellectual functioning, which originates during the developmental period (from before birth to age sixteen) and which is associated with impairments in physical maturation, social adjustment, and learning activities."

Mentally retarded or mentally handicapped persons are all ages and range in ability from mildly through profoundly retarded. Retardation has no respect for ethnic background or social status. It is a condition, not a disease, that can occur before, during, or after birth. It can be hereditary, but in most instances is caused by an accident, poor nutrition, abuse, drugs or alcohol during pregnancy, lack of oxygen, high fever, or other factors that are unknown. While research has helped us discover many reasons for retardation, most retardation cannot be traced to readily identifiable causes.

Many retarded persons will always need special help, but more will blend into society when they no longer have to cope with school. These individuals will live alone or with minimal help, hold a job, and may marry and have children. Retarded persons should not be stereotyped; they are unique individuals as all of us are. Retardation is a dynamic, not a static condition; retarded persons change and grow just as we do.

This chart briefly looks at levels of mental retardation and some of the characteristics at each level. Labels should not be used as the only means of identifying a person, though referring to a level of retardation helps people understand how well the individual can function. While an I.Q. score can be a help in determining a person's functioning level, it is only one factor to be considered.

LEVEL OF RETARDATION	CHARACTERISTICS
Profound (I.Q. 0-19)	Gross retardation. Minimal capability of developing sense and motor skills. Needs nursing care. Shows basic emotional responses. May learn to use legs, hands, jaws to some extent—walking, limited speech. Incapable of self-maintenance.
Severe (I.Q. 20-35)	Marked delay in motor development. Can learn elementary self-help (e.g., self-feeding, toileting). Usually walks if there is no physi-

LEVEL OF RETARDATION	CHARACTERISTICS
	cal disability. Has some understanding of speech and some response. Can follow daily routine and repetitive activities. Needs continuing supervision in a protective environment.
Moderate (I.Q. 36-52)	Noticeable delays in motor development, especially in speech. Can learn self-help skills, simple communication, health and safety habits, simple manual skills. Seldom learns reading, writing, or arithmetic to any great degree but can progress to about second-grade level. Can perform simple tasks in a sheltered environment. Has some degree of independence but will always need to rely on others.
Mild (I.Q. 53-75)	Often not noticed as retarded until school age, but is slower to walk, feed and talk than most children. Can acquire many practical skills. Can learn to read and do arithmetic at between third- and sixth-grade level in special classes. Can live semi-independently or independently with occasional guidance and support.
Slow Learner (I.Q. 76-99)	Not usually considered mentally retarded. Has difficulty in school but is usually in a regular classroom. Emotional and social difficulties may arise because of academic stress.

The purpose of this essay has not been to give you all the facts, although some have been imparted. It should say something to your heart; it should help you understand how parents of a retarded child feel and challenge you to think how you might respond to or help them.

SUGGESTIONS FOR FURTHER ACTION

1. Spend some time in quiet reflection on your own handicapping conditions and how you'd like others to respond to you.
2. Check with your parish council, one of the parish committees, the DRE, or your pastor to see if the needs of mentally handicapped and other disabled parishioners are being met. This includes things such as wheelchair accessibility and special religious education classes.
3. Contact your local Association for Retarded Citizens (ARC) for more information about retardation.
4. Seek out a parent of a retarded child to learn more about how that child affects the family. This can be done through the local ARC or perhaps by contacting a special education teacher in your school district.
5. Invite parents of retarded children to come to a parish meeting to discuss what the church can do for them.
6. Visit a residential facility for retarded persons or a group home. Check with the administrator to see if you can entertain or visit, or for suggestions on what to do while you're there.

BRIGID O'DONNELL. Ms. O'Donnell holds an M.A. in Religious Studies from Mundelein College in Chicago. She is Associate Director of Religious Education in the Diocese of Madison, specializing in the areas of family and special education.

MINISTRY TO THE DYING

Rev. Donald G. McCarthy

Television, radio, and newspapers confront us day after day with news of death: executions, bombings, plane crashes, Legionnaire's disease, the ravages of cancer, and the regular accounts of auto crashes. Yet these deaths are unreal for many of us.

For example, a newspaper account recently told of a child who shot a playmate, fatally injuring him. The child showed no sorrow or regret.

"Don't you realize," his distraught mother asked him, "that little Bruce is *dead*? That he'll never walk or talk or play again?"

"Who said so?" the boy retorted. "I see guys getting killed every day on TV, and the next day they're playing on another show."

Admittedly, adults appreciate more realistically the finality of death, yet our American culture has treated death in a notably impersonal and artificial style. Over two-thirds of those who die in the United States do so in a hospital or nursing home where the body is immediately covered and discreetly transferred to the secluded sanctuary of a funeral home. If the body is viewed later before burial it will be made to "look alive," complete with eyeglasses, hair styling, and makeup.

Even the horrors of death in two World Wars and the Korean War were far enough away for the American people to maintain their composure. Twentieth-century medical progress, miracle drugs, amazing new medical equipment, and even organ transplants have supported our complacent denial of death.

Only in the past decade has a more sober realization of death taken hold of the American psyche. Perhaps it began with the tragedy of Vietnam—the first war brought to us "live" on television. Maybe the mood of the 1960s prepared us to face death, the mood of the social activists and the hippies who despised hypocrisy and the establishment.

The person who began awakening our whole nation to death and dying is Dr. Elisabeth Kübler-Ross, the dynamic Swiss-born psychiatrist who was listening to the dying in Chicago and began publishing her findings in 1969.

More recently the nation has seen the dilemma of indefinitely forestalling death without hope of return to consciousness in the sad case of Karen Ann Quinlan. The prospect of powerful medical professionals using a technological toolbox to force patients into prolonged dying has won nationwide support for "death with dignity." Most state legislatures have been considering legislation to guarantee the so-called "right to die."

The Church, meanwhile, carries the responsibility, according to the Second Vatican Council, of "reading the signs of the times and interpreting them in the light of the Gospel." Catholic Christianity recognizes the evil of suffering and death, and resists that evil by reasonable medical efforts. But, ultimately, both the Church and the Gospels call Christians to endure suffering and death with Christ in order to rise with him.

The current cultural preoccupation with the dignity of death demands a parallel and profound preoccupation with the dignity of Christian death in the family and the parish community. How can we offer Christian ministry to the dying today?

MINISTRY TO THE DYING

This ministry cannot properly begin until both the dying person and the family acknowledge to each other the approach of death. Then comes the challenge of experiencing death in the light of faith. Each of these two themes will be discussed.

Facing Death in the Family

Despite the amazing progress of modern medicine and the efficient skills of hospitals and nursing homes, the Grim Reaper gathers a regular harvest, but now two-thirds of those who die are over sixty-five years of age. With improved skills in neonatal care and handling children's diseases, only about one death in twenty is a child under fifteen years of age.

This medical progress has thus delayed the approach of death and even provided some cancer cures. Yet this contributes to the fiction in which family members maintain false hopes for the recovery of dying persons and avoid speaking of death.

Doctors themselves have been known to participate in elaborate conspiracies to shield their patients from the grim news of impending death. In a survey published in a well-known medical journal in 1961, for example, 90 percent of the physicians indicated their preference for not telling a cancer patient his or her diagnosis.

The decade since Dr. Elisabeth Kübler-Ross began her study of death and dying has seen an amazing shift in the willingness of physicians to communicate a terminal diagnosis. In fact, the same survey used in 1961 was repeated in 1977 with 97 percent of the physicians now preferring to tell a cancer patient his or her diagnosis!

Actually, most dying persons realize they are dying, even when the subject is not discussed. One physician pointed out that when they are not told verbally they are told through "voiceless messages that are as loud as shouts through a megaphone." They read the sad expressions on visitors' faces and they sense the gloom that is covered with only a brittle facade.

Hence an honest recognition that an illness may be terminal seems generally necessary for authentic ministry to the dying. Ill persons can feel cruelly isolated by the conspiracy of silence about their illness. Even those who prefer not to discuss it have effectively isolated themselves by this withdrawal. A pregnant woman who could not discuss her condition would be isolated by that barrier—a dying person far more so.

Sometimes dying persons avoid discussing their condition to shield spouses and family members from the pain of impending separation. Yet this separation is inevitable and dying persons find great peace after it has been acknowledged.

Family members often find the reality of death disagreeable not only because of impending separation but because they have not accepted their own mortality. Hence the honest recognition of terminal illness can become a growth experience for the family as well as the dying person.

Dr. Kübler-Ross has outlined five stages through which dying persons usually pass, moving from denial and anger into bargaining with God and then depression and, finally, acceptance. Family members who care for a dying person will often participate in these same stages. Kübler-Ross's work helps everyone recognize them and thereby deal with their feelings more effectively.

Within a family one indication of readiness to face death is the way children are taught honestly about it. Families in which children are shielded from attending funerals or in which the parents are unwilling to discuss what happens after death will find it hard to minister to a dying person.

On the other hand, parents who discuss death openly with their children, perhaps on the occasion of the death of a pet animal or of a televised funeral, have progressed beyond the denial of death so common in our culture.

Many people hesitate to talk about death because it raises the mysterious religious questions of judgment and life after death. Even those who have accepted the answers that Christian faith provides for these questions often find themselves uncomfortable because they cannot speak from any experience of judgment and life after death.

Death in the Light of Faith

The Catholic faith teaches us to view suffering and death within a vision of the universe unattainable by human reason alone. Human experience testifies readily enough to birth, growth, suffering, and death, but what is the meaning and purpose of life and the reason for physical and moral evil?

The Catholic faith does not insist that ours is the best of all possible worlds, as some philosophers have supposed. But it does insist on the loving goodness of God despite the evil in the world. It explains evil through original sin, the hereditary alienation of the human family from God with its attendant exposure to disease and corruption, and through personal sin, the use of human freedom contrary to human goodness and fulfillment.

Hence suffering and death are as real and as destructive for Christians as for anyone else, but with a difference. Christians believe that the God who permits evil does not abandon his people to face it alone. On the contrary, the life, suffering, death, and resurrection of Jesus established his victory over suffering, evil, and death. This is redemption.

Faith teaches that whereas death came into the world through human disobedience and rejection of divine love, for Christ death became a sign of love and submission to his Father. Christians unite themselves with Jesus so that their suffering and death participate in that love and redemption.

If Christ would stand at the bedside of all dying persons, they would surely experience hope and courage. Instead he stands there in the Christian community, both priests and laity, who keep the bedside vigil. The Christian meaning of suffering and death, like faith itself, comes to people through the Church.

In fact, suffering and death are not the only elements of life to be experienced with Christ. The core meaning of every event in life flows from living that event through Christ, with Christ, and in Christ. This love story of human life in Christ transforms the lonely anxiety of the pagan without faith into the hopeful optimism of the Christian family in joy and in sorrow, in pleasure and in pain.

Christ touches his people directly and intimately in the Sacraments, especially in the heavenly food of the Eucharist. Dying persons need that food, called viaticum or travelers' food, as well as the strength and consolation of the Anointing of the Sick.

The fears of dying persons include fear of pain, fear of separation and the unknown, and fear of divine judgment. Ministry to the dying includes the most competent pain control possible, but it must also face the other problems. Happily, once dying persons have placed themselves totally in God's hands, their fears of aloneness and judgment can be overcome.

The center of every person's moral life can be focused only on either God or some substitute good. Those who choose God enjoy the gift of grace, which is the pledge of future glory. Hence the secret of a good death rests in a continual deepening of that choice so that it becomes the final option when one is called by Christ to the Father. Those whose lives have been marked by selfishness and neglect of grace need a deepening conversion that often occurs and becomes evident. Without that conversion, the fear of divine judgment continues to haunt dying people.

Family members who care for dying persons have unique opportunities to give spiritual assistance. The love of Christ at the core of Christian life finds its first human expression in family love. In fact, those who are starved for human love find it hard to appreciate divine love. Conversely, those who express authentic human love testify to divine love. Family love and reconciliation facilitate conversion to divine love and peace.

Furthermore, family members know better than anyone the moral struggles the dying person has experienced. They know better what the weaknesses have been that must be repented and redeemed in preparation for death. Their own warmth, understanding, and forgiveness can symbolize the warmth, understanding, and forgiveness of the Father in heaven.

Yet such basic attitudes of love and support do not exhaust the spiritual assistance family members should give to dying persons. If the dying should "know Christ and his power" and "share in his sufferings," Christ must be acknowledged in the sickroom. Families who are accustomed to pray together will readily pray the Good Shepherd Psalm (23), the Lord's prayer, and the rosary. Many people today have discovered how to pray aloud spontaneously. Family members can take that initiative much more comfortably than visitors.

Within a family the experience of ministering to a dying person should be roughly equivalent to making a retreat—a time of prayerful and shared reflection on the great mysteries of life and God's love.

CONCLUSION

The two discussions presented here can be united into one basic theme: facing a family death in the light of faith. This theme presents a challenge in family healing—one that may be more easily met by Christians today because of a greater cultural openness today about death and dying. Everything said about the family's ministry to the dying member applies analogously to the parish family and its ministry to dying parishioners.

Christians have always believed that death is not defeat because life is changed, not ended. In this conviction they are more likely to forego extraordinary means of prolonging life without losing reverence for life or falling into the trap of mercy killing or inducing death to escape suffering.

Facing death honestly in the family with the light of faith will greatly diminish the burdens of grief after death. The family unity, although interrupted by death, continues as an abiding unity in Christ and in his promise of a glorious reunion in heaven.

In essence, then, ministry to the dying means making room for our loved ones to die with Christ.

REV. DONALD G. MCCARTHY. Father McCarthy has a doctorate in Philosophy from the University of Louvain. He is a priest of the Archdiocese of Cincinnati where he teaches at Mt. St. Mary Seminary. He held a Fellowship in Theology and Medical Ethics at the Institute of Religion in the Houston Medical Center.

FACING ECONOMIC PROBLEMS IN THE FAMILY

Maureen Miller

They come from various walks of life, economic levels, and professions, and they are joined by a common bond. They face economic problems that affect not only them but their entire family.

There is Betty—with $140.00 left in her checking account and $1000.00 left in savings, out of work, hoping desperately to get that $3.00 an hour job, worrying about not having health insurance for herself and her 12-year-old son. And Ella, on welfare, saying, "Until a year and a half ago, I managed real well, but now I can't make it. At mid-month, I have only $17.00 left."

There is Lara who tells of tossing and turning through the night wondering if she should lend money to a grown child caught in a revolving cycle of loan company payments. And Fred, buying powdered milk, getting into his ten-year-old car purchased from his sister several years ago, going to his modest apartment after a ten-hour day at work (that ranks him in the 50% taxable income bracket), figuring out how to meet the college expenses of his children. And there is Frank, saying, "It's the grocery store that's the biggest monster. That and gasoline. The other purchases are not so frequent. We do not have to face them every day."

Real-life problems. Typical problems. The kind one might meet at any time. And yet, behind them lurks a more pervasive worry, a sense "of not knowing what might come next." It is not just having particular money concerns but of facing them in a time when an inflation rate soared to 13% in three months of a new year; of salaries not keeping up with the pace of advancing prices; of over 6.2 billion dollars spent for food stamps for over 19 million people (an increase of over 4.5 million people in less than six months). It is an end-of-a-decade time when the buying power of a dollar has been cut in half in the past eleven years, and the elderly on fixed incomes face a reality that can snuff out hopeful dreams made ten years earlier. It is dealing with present problems while also not knowing where the times are taking us. And it all combines to cut even more deeply the wounds that all economic problems make on life.

Persistent money worries make incisions difficult to heal because there are no exact dimensions on their scope or effect. It isn't just present set-backs that affect us but the fact that they radiate to all areas of life. They aggravate other stresses. They can nag away at our thinking and chip away at productivity. They can cause fatigue and worry that spawns unrelated arguments. They can cause disagreements of such a nature that problems over money make up one of the main causes of divorce.

Handling and healing deep financial problems is not easy, not only because they affect other areas in our lives but because they are coupled with deeply ingrained attitudes and values about ourselves and our life. Healing is not easy, but it can be accomplished. This is the purpose of this essay: to help us see ways of meeting economic problems. Here we will look more closely at the climate of concern; at common causes and remedies for money troubles; at community and legal resources that can help us; and at individual ways of coping with financial troubles.

THE CLIMATE OF CONCERN

The foreboding sense of not knowing what is coming next pervades the texture of our lives. It is in the voice of one astute businessman talking to another: "Something is bound to happen." It is in the thinking of the mother: "One might as well buy now; you might not be able to do so later—things might just cost so much more."

And it is in the deep concern of Frank (who faces the grocery store monster): "It is a constant burden I endure, not knowing what is going to happen. I don't panic, but neither do I meet this with acceptance. This is much harder to deal with than a tangible hurt. I can deal with something absolute. If there is something that is going to happen, I would rather it happen; I can deal with what is expected. All I know is that each time I go to the grocery store, I can expect things to be higher."

Frank continued to stress the "worse problem—not knowing what is coming." As he said, "I think it is symptomatic of our entire culture. It is not a separate part, but an identifiable part of other things over which we have no control. This, I think, is a bigger worry. A lack of dollars in one's billfold is the most imminent worry, but it may not be the most important. Not knowing what to expect is lacking a power to control our lives. And lack of control over what is happening economically is part of our overall lack of control over other aspects of our lives. It is what makes some people turn to violence."

ECONOMIC PROBLEMS: SOME CAUSES AND REMEDIES

Although there is little to help us know what is coming next, there are very definite things we can do to face this "not knowing" and accompanying financial problems. There are areas in our life we can control or modify. We can examine our views of self and our way of managing money.

OUR NEEDS, ATTITUDES AND VALUES

The way we use money reflects not only rational decisions but complex emotional patterns, attitudes about ourselves and life, and our inner needs. Because we are motivated by our needs, it is good to look at those which can influence the way we spend money. They include the physiological needs for food, shelter, clothing, safety, love and belonging, self-esteem, and self-fulfillment. We can examine our patterns of spending money, try to see the motivating factor behind them, and see if any factor adversely affects our money behavior. If so, we can try to modify such behavior and its underlying cause.

Take the way we think of ourselves, for instance. A lack of self-esteem can lead us to think that our sense of worth depends on our possessions. With such an attitude we can easily be lured into the entrapments of overbuying to find happiness. When we discover that such happiness is illusory, we can be led to more buying in a desperate search to feel good about ourselves. The cycle continues. Our momentary pleasure becomes an addictive merry-go-round ride which, although it may make us dizzy, is hard to give up.

Not knowing what we really value (or failing to stop long enough to sort out our needs and wants from those of our friends or societal trends) can cause a similar dissatisfaction. We end up with things that really don't seem ours. We have no internal satisfaction, only a superficial feeling of "showing someone else," or of "showing up someone else."

The solution cannot come overnight, but we can steadily work at it. We can resolve to think about who we are, what our wants and needs are, to value ourselves, our strengths, dignity and worth as individuals, and to sort out our real values throughout the days, not just on a last-minute decision in a hurry-up jaunt to the newest shopping center. We can say to ourselves, "In buying, I will think of my wants and needs and those of my family. I will not let my wants exceed my needs." We can tell ourselves (as I heard a father advise his pre-school son): "Talk to your brain."

Money management: "Talk to your brain." The advice is also excellent to overcome poor money management. We can use this advice in dealing with three areas: our use of credit; keeping records; and careful purchasing.

Our use of credit: Our billfolds bulge with the credit cards that make buying so easy. Using credit cards has strong advantages: we have good records of purchases; we do not have to carry large sums of money; proper use can give us good credit rating. But their availability also makes it easy to get caught up in their abuse: a buy-now-and-pay-later cycle that can spin so fast that before we know it we are taking the phone off the hook so the creditors can't call us while we juggle paying the accounts to stay ahead of the game.

One "before-the-fact" solution consists in paying the balance of credit card debts monthly to avoid the average 18% interest rate. Remember that money owed at 18% interest almost doubles in 5 years and if we owe a continuing balance of $1000.00, we are using up almost the same amount in interest alone. We can also keep our borrowing on an even keel by keeping in mind what experts in money management tell us: Excluding house payments, do not owe more than 20% of yearly, after-tax income. Monthly debts should not exceed 10% of our monthly take-home pay; our debts should not exceed one-third of the money we have left after basics such as food, housing, and clothing have been taken care of.

Keeping records is vital to good money management. Knowing how much money is coming in and going out can help us keep out and get out of debt, and also set goals for what we really want. It takes very little to keep adequate records: pencil, notebook, envelopes for receipts, and one general place to keep all records. Whatever plan we use, records should be simple and used with discipline. As a woman recalled, "When I found out how much in debt we were, I was really shocked. I got a ledger, recorded absolutely every purchase and did not buy anything we did not need. Little by little, I managed to pay off our debts."

Generally speaking, there is no need to be that stringent on oneself. Basically, planning can follow this pattern: Record after-tax income; total all fixed expenses (rent, utilities, insurance, contract debts, etc.) including savings for an emergency fund; subtract that total from the total money coming in. What is left can be spent for flexible expenses such as food, clothing, entertainment, etc. Total the flexible expenditures and the fixed expenses, and subtract from the total money coming in. What is left can be used for short-range or long-range goals. Obviously, if the budget doesn't balance, adjustments in flexible spending (or even an extra job) will have to be made. A plan such as this can be charted for a twelve-month basis; it can be tried and adjusted accordingly.

In planning a budget, partners can remember that money has different values (in addition to monetary) for different people. Money and how it is used carries psychological impact: love, self-esteem, security, and freedom are among its main symbols and motivational forces for use.

Your money plan is a joint venture, and individual differences, natures, and values should be considered. A long distance telephone call versus cigarettes—each can seem a foolish expenditure to the opposite partner, but it is helpful to remember that the way we use money isn't always rational but carries emotional connotations. In working on a mutual plan, face money problems honestly (it helps to get them down on paper); compromise and work out differences in values; agree on a spending plan; stick to the budgeting and/or adjust it accordingly, and be sure to plan for personal allowances that do not have to be accounted for.

Buying wisely can pare down flexible spending allotments. Some helps are: watching for seasonal sales, buying seconds which do not detract from wearability, buying at discount stores and manufacturers outlets, avoiding overbuying (a $20.00 item reduced to $2.00 is not a bargain if you can't use the item), charting a plan to change unwise buying habits (such as compulsive buying).

Buying clothes and household items at garage sales and "gently-used" merchandise outlets, trading, borrowing, or renting seldom used items, and cutting down on the excessively-rising cost of services by learning do-it-yourself methods can also trim money outlays to a great degree and allow for saving toward short-range or long-range financial goals.

COMMUNITY AND LEGAL RESOURCES

Various measures can pare down expenses, help us face inflation, work toward goals and even solve financial crises. Often we can make it on our own. However, there are times when financial problems strike us with such force that it is difficult to think wisely. We operate through numbness in a fog of indecision that makes even knowing where to turn an almost impossible task.

When situations such as this arise we can look to others in the community by seeking help from our church ministry, a local United Way, or Social Services organizations which offer help or guidance in housing, food, shelter, and overall needs. If we are over sixty, we can see if Home Making Services, Home Care and Meals, or Congregate

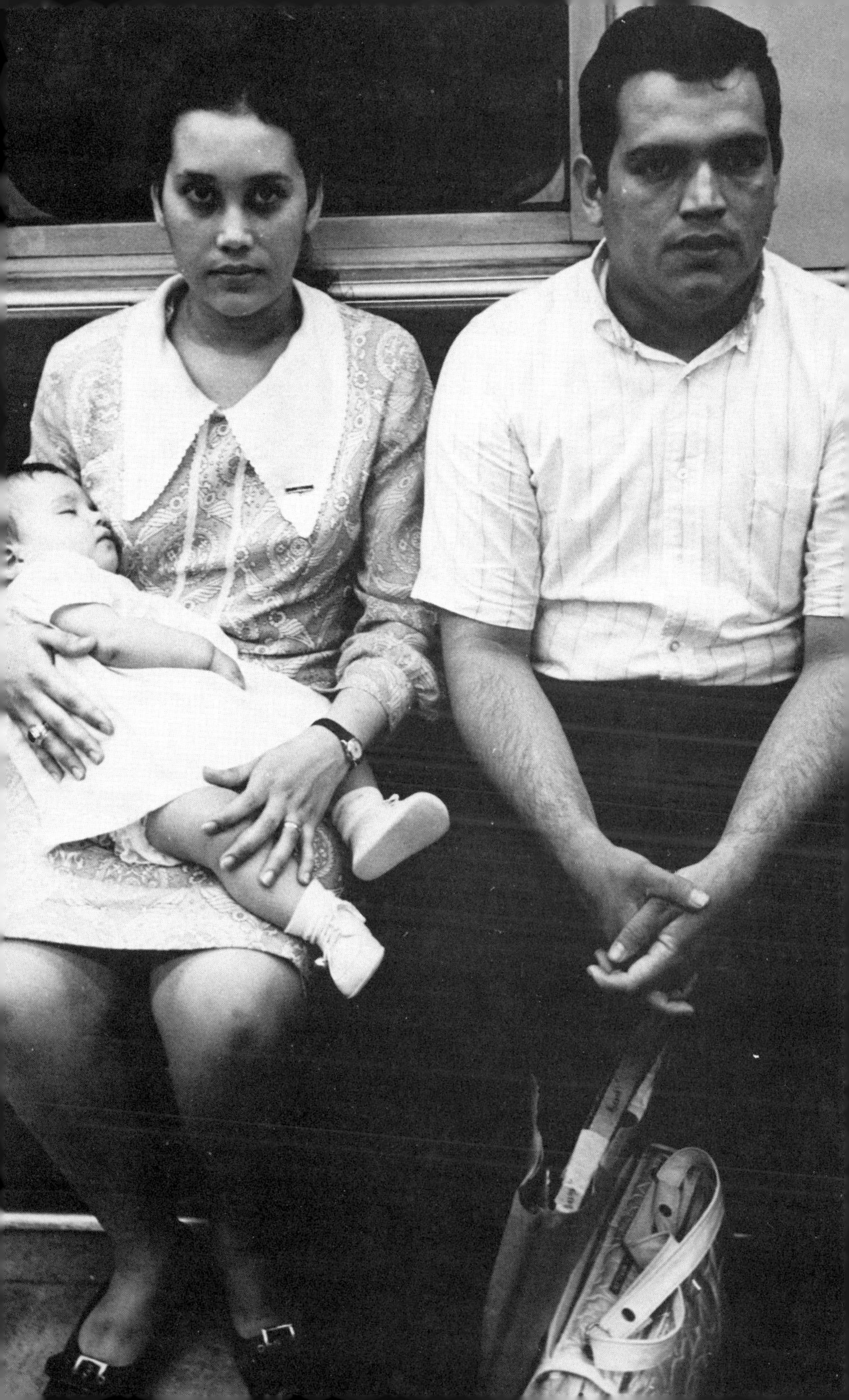

Meal Programs are available. Check with city government (City Hall) for the location of the nearest Community Development program that offers federally-funded services such as these offered in a midwest city: assistance in paying utility bills to those who meet certain low-income guidelines; food vouchers up to $250.00 for the elderly who have paid their utility bills regularly and can prove a declaration of need; and home repair programs. Phone or go to an Extension Service (operated in every county in every state of the nation) for assistance, including publications, in areas of family financing, basics of budgeting, and money management.

If one has become so enmeshed in a web of credit abuse and overspending and help is needed to get untangled, seek financial counseling from a Family Service Agency, Consumer Credit Counseling Service, or possibly your labor union, credit union, or church. (Or write the National Family Service Association of America, 44 East Twenty-third Street, New York, N.Y. 10010; or the National Foundation for Consumer Credit, 1819 H Street, Washington, D.C. for the location of the nearest counselor.)

You can also reorganize your debts under the Wage Earner Plan. This is not bankruptcy, but a provision of the Federal Bankruptcy Law which shows creditors you are in good faith in wanting to pay off creditors. In this plan, under the supervision of a federal judge, you meet with creditors (half of creditors must approve of your action) and a trustee to work out a way in which you can pay off your debts in installments. You give the money for these payments to a trustee who in turn parcels it out to creditors. The advantages are that creditors are held at bay and cannot bother you; collection activities stop; interest on the unpaid portion of the debts stop; unsecured debts are prorated out (your home mortgage, for instance, is a secured debt). If you run into a disaster, you will have someone to intervene for you; you escape bankruptcy; and if you succeed at paying off your debts, this positively affects your credit rating.

A new bankruptcy act goes into effect on October 1, 1979. As a legal expert explained, "This is a deliberate step to create a policy of treating the consumer as a person of dignity. Its emphasis is on protecting the debtor, particularly one who is sincere about wanting to get out of debt."

Resources to help those with financial problems differ according to communities, but positive help can be found through the above measures. Assistance can also be had through adult education classes and church-sponsored services. Two such services which can be adopted or modified according to the community are The Emergency Food Pantries, sponsored by the Des Moines (Iowa) Area Religious Council of Churches, and Mom's Day Out, an eight–twelve week series of classes including those dealing with consumer affairs, sponsored by the Home and Family Life Division of the Department of Community and Adult Education in Des Moines. (See Suggestions for Further Action for a further description of these services.)

INDIVIDUAL RESOURCES

It was as Betty recalled, "Well, you just make it through. When my husband left me, I was living in another state. For five days straight, I applied at a furniture factory near my home so I wouldn't have to use money for transportation. Finally, in desperation, I called there and said, 'I am out of money. I need the work. I can learn anything.' I was given a sanding job, didn't know anything about it, but just watched the person next to me. . . . Those first days, we planned our entertainment so that it wouldn't cost anything: walks on the beach, hunting for sharks teeth, and fishing. I buy my clothes at rummage sales and Goodwill Stores, and I can make my furniture from things other people throw away (a stand for my television set is a draped, backless chair, for instance)."

As high as his income is, Fred has to economize in various ways in his goal to get all of his children through college. "The thing is," he explained, "none of them can get any financial assistance because of my income. With as many as three in college at one time, it means paying about $15,000.00 a year in schooling costs. They work at summer jobs, and I get along on little myself. If things get bad, I can always live in one room. I don't need much for myself—books and music."

Lara's decision to lend the money to a child in a financial bind "is working out fine." She says, "I'm getting the same interest I could get if I invested it. I feel we are both helping one another."

And Ella, on welfare, plans how she is going to get along. "Bill, my oldest son, is coming home, and he's going to help with the groceries when he's here. Then in the fall, I think I will be getting a job."

Frank, who so insistently stressed the problem of not knowing what was coming next, also shows how much control his family exerts to save money: "We've changed the way we buy food; we think in terms of how many meals we will get from a certain buy of meat. A thirteen-pound ham at $1.29 a pound can last our family of five for twelve days. Maybe we even have more variety that way. It takes ingenuity to think of different ways to serve the same cut of meat.

"I also plan to ride a bike to work, and I eat lunch at home almost all of the time. My daughter takes her lunch to school, and that alone saves over $10.00 a month. We use food coupons, my wife makes some of her clothes, and I work an extra part-time job whenever I can. For the first time, we planted a garden, and we really look to that to save money. All of these things have two targets. We save money, and also relieve the psychological burden. These actions tell us we are doing something. We are in some way in control. . . . One thing, though, we really wanted to give my daughter piano lessons, but there is no way we can do that. We've had to give up that idea."

Giving up some things, doing whatever one can, eliminating purchased services, using creativity, determination, self-reliance—these are all part of meeting economic problems.

All of this contributes to a positive attitude about oneself. It joins with a plan of money management and the use of community resources to make it possible to say, "It might not be as we planned, but we can do more than just survive. As much as possible, we can be in control!"

SUGGESTIONS FOR FURTHER ACTION

Mom's Day Out is a unique program that offers free classes and workshops in consumer homemaking, home management, child development, parenting, and personal growth and development to Des Moines, Iowa mothers. Clientele is mainly composed of low-income mothers of pre-school children.

The 9:00 A.M. to 2:00 P.M. sessions, sponsored by the Home and Family Life Division of the Department of Community and Adult Education, include services dealing with budgeting, coping with stresses, and setting positive life goals. A special nursery is provided for pre-school children. Later plans include a therapeutic nursery with modeling by the staff of the Child Guidance Center to show mothers child management skills.

If problems of a special, individual economic nature come to light through these Mom's Day Out sessions, home economic outreach workers deal directly with the individual homemaker on budgeting, wise food planning, and personal home management skills.

Referrals to the program come from social service and community agencies, and part of the expenditures of the program (including those for materials and baby sitting services) are underwritten by the Polk County (Iowa) Department of Social Services.

This Mom's Day Out Program is part of overall services offered by the Department of Community and Adult Education which include consumer assistance in dealing with economic problems. The wide variety of adult education classes include estate planning, retirement, and medical insurance to persons over sixty. The Family Learning Centers, also operated by the Community and Adult Education, offer workshops in interpersonal relationships, communication skills, parenting, and parent-child educational needs. All combine to help the whole person. This, in turn, can help individuals change their attitudes and behaviors regarding economic needs and money management.

Emergency Food Pantries, sponsored by the Religious Council of Churches of Des Moines, Iowa, with one hundred thirteen participating congregations, is now completing its third year of operation. The pantries provide food to those in special need.

Six emergency stores are located in low-income areas of the city and are stocked with basic foods contributed by people throughout the community. On the one Sunday a month which is designated as Food Sunday, food is brought to local churches. From these locations, it is delivered to one room at the Central Administrative Offices of the Des Moines Religious Council, and from this location it is parceled out to the various centers.

Food pantries are designed for emergency food use, not as a continual source of food supply, and guidelines as to their use are flexible. However, an emergency must exist in each case of use. On visiting a center, a client can obtain food for a sound nutritional diet for a four to five day period of time. Food for diabetics and special infant formula needs is also available.

Records and cross-checking between stores prevent abuses. If the same family shows up for the second or third time, store personnel can guide it to various other social service agencies in the city. In this way, the whole person or whole family can be helped, thus alleviating problems that gave rise to the original economic plight.

Elderly residents can visit the food pantry as often as needed if the need is ascertained, and if there is no other means available for them to obtain food.

Initial promotion to launch the program included notices sent to all churches in the community and large-scale newspaper publicity. This is augmented with continuing promotion such as free public service television spots to keep the public informed about how they can help, as well as newsletter announcements made to participating members of the religious council.

MAUREEN MILLER. Mrs. Miller holds an M.S. in Journalism and Mass Communication from Iowa State University. She is a Family Learning Center Specialist for the Department of Community and Adult Education in Des Moines. Among her writings is *Family Communication: Keeping Connected in a Changing World*.

HEALING THROUGH PRAYER

Rev. Theodore E. Dobson

When many of us have problems, we tend to use a few favorite ways to solve them. For example, some people may be among the type who tend to worry over problems; somewhere down deep inside of them they feel that unless they fret and churn their insides, things will not come out right. Others may first put logic to use in attempting to solve problems; these see the world as a system of causes and effects that can be analyzed to find insights resulting in solutions, or they may be people who need to remain in control of their lives and see their intellects as keys to that control.

There are still others who tend to avoid problems; even the most heartbreaking of situations will be faced with a broad smile and an assurance to everyone that they are feeling fine, while deep within themselves, often unknown even to themselves, their hearts are aching with confusion or doubt or fear. Another type of person is the one who becomes angry whenever he or she is faced with difficulty or sorrow. Of course, the anger does not make the problem go away, but it can camouflage it quite well, especially for the person feeling the anger. But the difficulty or sorrow still exists beneath this foreboding layer of anger; and the anger accomplishes the task of assisting this person not to face the problem but rather to pretend it is really in the hands of someone else to solve.

As we read descriptions such as these, we may see ourselves in one or several of them, or they may spark within us an understanding of another kind of favorite way in which we meet daily problems. Not all ways of meeting life's difficulties are as destructive as those mentioned above—destructive in the sense that by using them a person cannot find a resolution to his or her problem, a person cannot find healing. So I need to ask myself, "When I am faced with a problem, what are the ways in which I first tend to react to it?"

When I worked in a parish, many people would come into my office exhibiting one or more of these or other destructive attitudes toward problems. After listening to their stories of frustration and confusion over the problems they were experiencing, and after listening to their tales of failure at solving these problems in the past and how angry they were over their failure, I began to suggest to them that as I read the Bible, God had a different plan for them. He did not want them to be caught up in these confusingly dangerous attitudes and feelings. Rather, he had a constructive direction for their lives, especially in the face of this difficulty. As Jesus told us so many times, for example, "Ask and you will receive, and your joy will be complete" (John 16:24). Down to the last person, each asked me, "How do I discover this direction God has for my life?" and to each of them I responded the same: "We must learn how to pray about this situation."

The focus of this essay, then, is learning a simple process by which to pray healing prayer. In the minds of some people, healing prayer is immediately connected with the charismatic renewal in the Church, and therefore is something with which they think they will be uncomfortable. The aim of this essay is to help us appreciate the fact that healing prayer is a natural form of praying. We all pray and ask God to help us; when he does help us we call that "healing." In this sense, healing prayer is nothing more than successful prayer, prayer that obtains what it seeks. And Jesus promised us that no less would be true: "Ask, and it will be given to you; search, and you will find; knock, and the door will be opened to you" (Matt. 7:7).

A second goal of this essay is to acquaint people with various dimensions of healing, e.g., the complexity of emotional healing; the importance of physical contact in healing prayer; the difference between prayer alone and prayer with others. None of these topics can be treated in depth, but the material dedicated to them is meant to convey as much simple, accurate, and clear information as space will allow.

A third goal will be to stimulate the reader to look at his/her emotional and spiritual reactions to the possibility of healing prayer in his/her own life for the problems existing right now. Much of the essay should touch people at this deeper level.

PRAYING FOR HEALING

Healing, especially healing of emotional or relational problems, comes from God. Whether we seek healing through science, wisdom, or prayer, its origin is in God. We know that our most direct contact with God is in prayer, and yet for many years now, people have been looking in every direction but prayer to find answers to their problems. Some have even seemed to have a prejudice against praying to find healing. But now, from many different directions, we find people who have tried many other methods and systems returning to prayer to find answers, hope, and the healing that they need.

The reason, of course, is that only God is the source of all we need—"Think of the flowers; they never have to spin or weave; yet I assure you, not even Solomon in all his regalia was robed like one of these" (Luke 12:27) as Jesus put it—and is waiting to share it with us as we learn to look on ourselves and our world from *his* point of view. Today we are finding people both professional and lay in medical, religious, psychological, and other helping fields turning to prayer as much as to the knowledge of science to find sources of life and wholeness for people in their pain. Since 1975 there has even been an organization called the Association of Christian Therapists dedicated to helping and encouraging professionals to learn how to use prayer in their professions.

And when we stop to think about it, does not this approach make perfect sense? It makes more sense than separating the healing that comes from God mediated through science, medicine, and human wisdom, and the healing that comes directly from him as a result of healing prayer.

THE BASIS OF HEALING PRAYER

Healing through prayer is nothing more than expecting God to be God. Which one of us, if we had a dear friend who was in trouble, and if we had the power to help him or her out of that trouble, would take the time and effort to do so? All of us, of course! And yet in our attitude toward prayer we often reveal the unconscious thought that God *would not* behave in just that way! From his own Word, however, we know that God loves us. The nature of love is active—love will not allow a person to sit back passively and see the beloved remain in pain. Love impels one to do something to relieve the pain of the one who is loved; and if we love deeply we will use all the power and energy we have to assist the beloved.

How much more will God, who is infinitely loving as well as infinitely powerful, help us whom he loves when we are in trouble? Many times Jesus tried to teach us this same truth, maybe most dramatically in the fifteenth chapter of the Gospel of Luke—the parables of the Lost Sheep, the Lost Coin, and the Lost Son.

HEALING IN ACTION

If God is Abba, loving and kind, and if he has revealed himself to the world in his son Jesus, the man who healed, affirmed, forgave, and selflessly spent his life for each person he met, then maybe we need to re-examine our notions about God and what he will do for us. Could it be that our thought that God might not love us enough to heal us is really our own attitude about ourselves—in other words, that we really do not love ourselves that much, and that if we were to be walking along a road and find ourselves in our condition of brokenness, we would pass ourselves by, saying we are not worth the time and effort it would take to help us? Maybe we need to learn to apply the parable of the Good Samaritan to ourselves as well as to others!

If God is willing and able to help us, and if we come to believe in the truth of his love, then only one thing more is necessary to find healing through prayer: learning how to do it. But just as it is difficult to come to the belief of a simple truth like "God loves me and will help to heal me" so also it is not an easy task to learn how to pray. Praying is simple but often not easy.

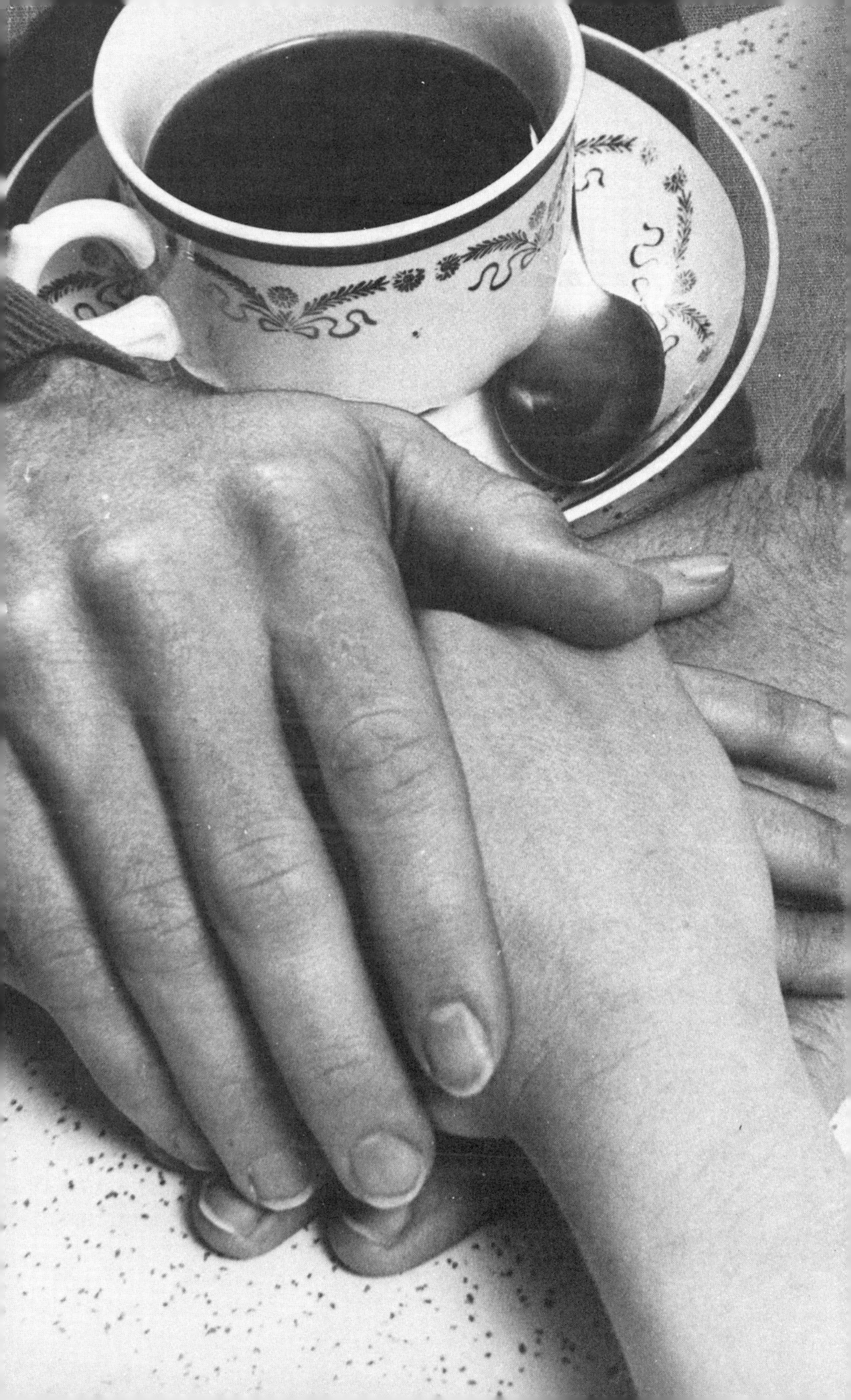

GUIDANCE—AN EXPRESSION OF LOVE

The place where all healing begins is seeking God's guidance. After all, it is *his* answer for our problem that we seek. Up to this point we have been trying to solve the problem our own way and have been using only human wisdom, and it has not worked. So we must stop trying to solve the problem on our own and seek *his* way. Many people, before reaching this point, say, "But I *have* prayed about this. I have prayed for God's help, but nothing has happened." We have prayed for his help to do *what*? Before we come to this point of yielding to God and admitting that he has the answers and healing we need, our prayers are often telling God how to solve the problem. We feel our prayers have not been answered because God has not done what we have told him to do. We have sought to impose our will on God, rather than try to discern what he wants for us.

Seeking God's guidance means becoming silent when it comes to requests, admonitions, directions aimed at God, and the like; it means listening and waiting. In this sense it is an expression of our love of God and our trust of his love for us. When I do not love another or trust his love of me I try to control his or her actions. Only in a relationship of love freely given and received can I become calm and listen to the other's—in this case God's—point of view.

REQUEST—AN EXPRESSION OF FAITH

God's guidance may come in many forms, e.g., an inner intuition, a word of wisdom from a friend, a seemingly chance circumstance, a line from Scripture that jumps out with meaning, a sudden insight coming in the midst of work, prayer, play, or sleep. I need to clarify first that this guidance is from God's Spirit and not some other source. Then I can move on to the second step, making my request. For now, in a real sense, the request I will make will not be "mine" alone, for the Spirit of God will have revealed to me what to ask for, and the request will be what Jesus requests for me. Having sought Jesus' will in my life and requesting it be done—"your kingdom come, your will be done, on earth (in my life) as in heaven" (Matt. 6:10)—I am praying in faith in the truest sense of that word.

The simplest way to pray in faith requesting of God that his will be accomplished in my life is by using my imagination. Jesus expressed it this way: "I will tell you, therefore: everything you ask and pray for, believe that you have it already, and it will be yours" (Mark 11:24). What better and simpler way is there to believe that I have received something already than to imagine that I have it? And if I have sought God's guidance and found out what his will intends me to have in this matter, then, as I request this gift from God and use my imagination to see that I have already received it, I am not creating some outlandish prayer, but rather I am putting my faith to hard work. "Only faith can guarantee the blessings that we hope for, or prove the existence of the realities that at present remain unseen" (Heb. 11:1). This is what is called "expectant faith," and when the object of this faith is God's will for us and not our own will for ourselves, it has the power to move mountains (Mark 11:22–23), mountains of problems, mountains of illness, mountains of despair.

First, we seek God's guidance—where does *he* want to begin to help and heal me? I seek him; I wait. I do not request anything specific until I receive some guidance about what he is doing in my life. In this way I place my problem entirely in his hands, trusting that if my problem is with him (and I do not take back responsibility for solving it by acting or praying prematurely), he is doing the most loving possible thing that can be done at this moment.

When I receive some insight into how God views my situation and what he is doing about it, I make my prayer of request, and, in loving detail, sense within me or visualize Jesus doing this very thing in my life. It could be that I see him bringing me and another person together, mending our relationship; it could be that I sense his presence within me loving me out of insecurity. It could be that he has shown me that this problem really started many years before I was aware of it, and he wants to come into that time in my life and heal the wound that is there by giving me a gift of concern or binding an emotional wound with understanding, peace, or compassion; or he may be ready to do one of a hundred other beautiful things. Whatever he does I accept as the best possible thing that could be done at this time. Often Jesus surprises me, however, by leading me quickly to an area I myself have never thought of as important to this problem, and in healing me in this area frees me peacefully but dramatically from my pain.

THANKS—AN EXPRESSION OF HOPE

But our prayer cannot stop here. Even after we pray through each detail of a situation seeing Jesus in it, we have yet one more important part of our prayer—thanking him. This is especially true in cases of deeply wounding or complicated problems, because rarely can they be healed in one prayer—just as a serious illness cannot be cured by one pill or a crippling neurosis healed in one visit to a psychologist. Therefore, we not only thank God for what he has done at the time of our first prayer, but we continue to thank him for healing during the days and weeks that follow until we see the situation resolved as he shows us he wants it resolved. This persistent, freely-chosen attitude of thanksgiving to God for what we do not yet see accomplished fully in our lives is the virtue of hope. "For we must be content to hope that we shall be saved—our salvation is not in sight, we should not have to be hoping for it if it were—but, as I say, we must hope to be saved since we are not saved yet—it is something we must wait for with patience" (Rom. 8:24–25).

Hope in thanksgiving is the way we help this sluggish physical world to "catch up" with the spiritual world. For when we prayed our prayer of request in faith we saw by the grace of God into the spiritual world and recognized what God was doing for us there. It may take some time for this physical world to feel the effect of that spiritual power fully; and, in the meantime, hope expressed in thanksgiving is our way of remaining open to the fullness of God's life coming into us.

LEVELS OF HEALING

If we expect to find healing through prayer for our problems, especially our marriage and family problems, which are often so complex, we need to understand that our problems—and therefore our healing—will be on ever deeper levels of our personalities.

The first level is insight; after I give up destructive ways to handle my difficulty I need to use the process of guidance–request–thanks to find true insight *from God* (not from introspection, which easily becomes an illness!) revealing the nature of my problem. This is the first and easiest level of healing. Next I will need to use the same process of guidance–request–thanks to understand the situation from the point of view of the others involved in it and to accept their point of view as valid.

Third, I will need to use the process again to find a willingness to communicate with those people and begin a more constructive dialogue with them based in love and trust. Fourth, I will need to use this process of guidance–request–thanks to find God's healing love for my wounded self and his forgiveness of my wrongdoing, shortsightedness, and sinfulness in this situation. Finally, and most importantly (and this is the most difficult but also the most beautiful and deepest level of healing), I use this process of healing prayer to allow the love and forgiveness of God to flow through me to others in my actions, not only in my words and thoughts. In this final step I am purified of my selfishness as I learn, with Jesus as my teacher, how to love other people in the way in which they can feel the love, not just in the way in which I feel comfortable in giving love.

PRAYING WITH OTHERS

All of us can think of situations in our lives in which we would be able to pray in this way on our own. Also, because we are twentieth-century Americans and individuality is so important to us, many people have a predisposition to doing many things alone—especially praying, because it is such a personal activity. Yet Jesus often encouraged us to pray with each other. "For where two or three meet in my name, I shall be there with them" (Matt. 18:20).

There are times, situations, and types of problems in which we are indeed better off to ask someone else to pray with us—not only *for* us but *with* us. This is especially true when our problems are so big, depressing, or confusing that we know we do not have enough faith, hope, and love to pray for ourselves. But also, even with more ordinary problems, we can benefit from someone else's point of view, support in faith, and power of prayer. Sometimes it is good not to have to struggle so hard with our problems alone, and the assistance in prayer of one or several friends makes our prayer for healing easier and more enjoyable.

And Jesus says that there is a special kind of power when we pray together for each other. Maybe that is true because when we pray with each other we are loving each other and thus calling Jesus willfully into our midst.

LAYING ON OF HANDS

Praying with another person can be as simple as first talking over the concern that needs prayer to get some understanding of it, then placing our hand gently on the person's head, shoulder, or arm, or holding their hands, and verbalizing the prayer of expectant faith as described above. The physical contact that is suggested is not an unimportant point. First of all, it is scriptural: all through the Acts of Apostles, as well as in many of the healing stories from Jesus' life, some form of physical contact, sometimes called "laying on of hands," was integral to the healing process. Secondly, and just as importantly, it is a gesture that comforts and reassures in a warm, human way the person with whom we are praying in his or her moment of need.

This kind of praying with others and laying on of hands can be done in almost any context, no matter how formal or informal—spouses praying together at night or at the start of a day, parents praying with children, people meeting in a small group, as a part of the Eucharist, a priest praying with a layperson in the Sacrament of Reconciliation or in an anointing service. We even see this kind of physical contact as an integral part of three sacraments—Confirmation, Anointing the Sick, and Holy Orders. As we learn to use laying on of hands as an ordinary tool of prayer, we will see why it is an ancient form of prayer, for the power of our faith, hope, and love will increase through this practice.

CONCLUSION

This process of expectant faith (guidance–request–thanks), coupled with an openness to pray with others and laying on of hands, can be applied to the five levels of healing in relationships mentioned above. When this is done, fantastic results and positive changes in lives have resulted. People who are faithful to this scripturally-based teaching find their lives becoming more whole and free, loving, forgiving, and creative. And that is the promise Jesus made to all of us: "I have come so that they may have life, and have it to the full" (John 10:10).

SUGGESTIONS FOR FURTHER ACTION

1. As parents pray with their children at night they might focus on the problems the child has had that day, but using the guidance–request–thanks process in simple words. Children understand this easily and will begin to pray with you because their faith is trusting. This kind of prayer could be applied especially to problems the child and parent have had with each other. Physical contact will be especially important to make the child feel comfortable, loved, and accepted, and in some situations embracing the child while praying with him or her could be most appropriate.
2. In the same manner, spouses can pray with each other at the beginning or end of the day about problems and worries, and especially the concerns they have in their own relationship. Using the guidance–request–thanks process and physical contact in the form of holding hands or some kind of embrace would be key elements to the success of this prayer.
3. With the priest of your parish (or, to work on a smaller scale, with the leader of some parish organi-

zation—parents' association, women's or men's club, religious education program—planning for that particular group) plan a simple, nonsacramental penance or anointing service, using some or all of these ideas: a) opening hymn and/or prayer; b) Scripture reading (e.g., Mark 11:20–26; John 14:11–14; Luke 18:15–17; Luke 7:36–50; Mark 16:14–20); c) homily aimed at encouraging people to believe that Jesus cares and heals; d) a general prayer of healing is prayed spontaneously or read prayerfully; e) with several priests, deacons, or other parish leaders in the sanctuary, invite people to come forward and simply state their need; the minister will anoint them, lay hands on them, and pray simply that God meet their need; during this time background music can be played; f) closing prayer and/or song.

4. A personal touch to add to the service described above in 3. is to use the blessing from the Roman Ritual for nonsacramental oil for use by laity in healing prayer. (See below.) Before the service, the oil is poured into small, watertight containers (easily available from a pharmacist) and placed on trays on the altar. The oil is blessed after the homily (c) and before the general prayer for healing (d) and then distributed to people when they are in the sanctuary for individual prayer. During the homily the homilist explains how oil is a sign of healing, how this oil is not for the Sacrament of the Sick but for use by laity at any time, and how using the oil at home can be a way to continue the effect of this service in the days and weeks to come.

BLESSING OF OIL, FOR USE BY LAITY.*

Our help is in the name of the Lord,
R. Who made heaven and earth.
EXORCISM
God's creature, oil,
I cast out the demon from you by God the Father almighty +
who made heaven and earth and sea and all
that they contain.
Let the adversary's power, the devil's legions,
and all Satan's attacks and machinations
be dispelled and driven afar from this creature, oil.
Let it bring health in body and mind to all who use it,
in the name of God + the Father almighty,
and of our Lord Jesus Christ + his Son,
and of the Holy Spirit + the Advocate,
as well as in the love of the same Jesus Christ our Lord,
who is coming to judge both the living and the dead
and the world by fire. R. Amen.
Lord, heed my prayer. R. And let my cry be heard by you.
The Lord be with you. R. And also with you.
Let us pray.
Lord God almighty,
before whom the hosts of angels stand in awe
and whose heavenly service we acknowledge,
may it please you to regard favorably
and to bless and hallow this creature, oil,*
which by your power has been pressed from the juice of olives.
You have ordained it for anointing the sick, so that,
when they are made well, they may give thanks to you,
the living and true God.
Grant, we pray, that those who use this oil,
which we are blessing + in your name,
may be delivered from all suffering, all infirmity,
and all wiles of the enemy.

---

* *The Roman Ritual,* transl. by Philip Weller (Milwaukee: Bruce, 1964), p. 573.
*The oil is sprinkled with holy water.

Let it be a means of averting any kind of adversity from man,
made in your image and redeemed by the precious blood of your Son,
so that he may never again suffer the sting of the ancient serpent,
through Christ our Lord. R. Amen.

REV. THEODORE E. DOBSON. Father Dobson holds a Master of Divinity Degree from St. Mary of the Lake Seminary (Illinois) and has been a member of the healing ministry since 1972. His writings on the healing ministry include *Inner Healing: God's Great Assurance* (Paulist Press).